MEMORIES AND MOVING ON

How I Survived Retirement

MARGARET NYHON

Willow Press

© Copyright 2020 Margaret Nyhon

Margaret Nyhon asserts her moral right to be identified as the author of this work.

All rights reserved. No part of this publication may be produced or transmitted in any form or by any means, electronic or mechanical, including photocopying, recording or information storage and retrieval systems, without permission in writing from the copyright holder.

Published by Willow Press

Contact author: margaretf@hotmail.co.nz

A catalogue record for this book is available from the National Library of New Zealand.

*'Our personal collections
are our life's reflections'*

Where do we begin?!

What are treasures? Collections of wealth, gold and jewels. No, not those treasures, these ones: cherished things that we cling to, care for, things that bring back memories, some happy, some sad, in other words a mixture of emotions that makes up what is called 'life'.

Our impulses to collect and hold on to things can sometimes be driven purely by our emotions. Our possessions can embody our memories or can be a motivator reminding us of our hopes and dreams, our special moments in time, as we are about to find out.

We will begin with our wedding photo, the one I look at every morning that hangs forlornly on our bedroom wall. It seems to want to move, as I am forever straightening it to make it look just that little bit respectable. Perhaps it thinks it has had its day but I have news for it: it is staying where it belongs! This very photo reminded me of the biggest gossip session in my home town many years ago.

What happened to that lovely young girl from the garden shop? The one that served all the old folk when they came for gardening advice on what to grow at certain times of the year. She along with her father were their lifeline; she listened to all their stories, sometimes wishing they were just sentences, instead of everlasting histories. But she had been brought up to respect and listen to her elders. She always carried their purchases to their cars, or packed them in their baskets so they arrived home safely.

Suddenly, out of the blue she disappeared with no mention of what might have happened to her. No one liked to ask the father in case of offending him. Then one day all was revealed: she had taken the path to purgatory! It circulated the town like wildfire, hot on the trail from one gossiper's home to the next, leaving the townspeople speechless and very judgemental. The source of the information had come from one of the town's most well-known gossips. Her daughter worked in the manual telephone exchange and had eavesdropped on a phone call to one of her mother's friends. It went like this: "Myrtle, I must tell you what I have just seen, I had to tell someone. The young girl from the garden shop, I have just seen her, she is staying in a motel next to us in Nelson with a strange young man. I enquired at reception and they have registered as Mr and Mrs. Fancy having the audacity pretending to be married. That is why she is not at the garden shop any more." This was indeed hot off the press, thus having to be relayed back to her bosom friends; now she would be top of the pops in her gossip circle!

But unbeknown to these busybodies, whose lives were as narrow as an English country lane and who thrived on other people's misdemeanours, we were indeed a newly married couple who had eloped and married in a registry office. We were honeymooning in Nelson and we were both of legal age, and now of legal married status. But for the gossipmongers, it was a feast! It was easier for them to presume, rather than find the actual facts. This is what kept them alive, they thrived on gossip; it kept their so-called brains occupied.

Then one day, the young girl appeared back in the shop. Had her father fetched her home? Had she redeemed herself? So many unanswered questions. No one dared ask. Meanwhile our honeymoon was over and we had decided to let nature take care of itself, thus choosing not to use contraceptives, and as the months passed, it became noticeable that I was indeed pregnant and couldn't do much to hide my expanding waistline. So, the flames were re-ignited ... the poor girl, was she pregnant? Is that why she had been brought home? The tongues were at it again. The big question now was when was the baby due? The calendars were marked in anticipation of an early birth. Those ladies of the gossip circle couldn't believe when nine months came and went and still no baby. What had happened? They were disappointed as they had been let down. Now it was time to switch their focus to their next victim. They needed the gossip; how else were they going to fill in their day?

Back to our only wedding photo, which was taken on the day with an Instamatic camera, outside the registry office. The photo was developed straight away, so the quality was not of great clarity. As the years passed, the photo had faded. It was on our bedroom wall because it was not one to be proud of to show to friends; but to my soul mate and myself it signified our defiance and determination to be together as lovers, against all odds! The odds being religion, nothing else.

In February we celebrated our fifty-fifth wedding anniversary, so yes, we survived the gossip and hardships, the laughter and the tears, the good and bad times and now in sickness and in health! We have climbed the highest mountain together (figuratively speaking) and conquered it. It was a test of endurance, it wasn't easy, but since then, I have learnt life wasn't meant to be easy. It is a challenge sent to us all; some can handle it, others fall by the wayside. We never gave up, we were survivors!

Now on with my story. Growing older; no, what I really meant to say, as we mature and the years pass us by, we experience life, we accumulate treasures, things we can't part with, because they are the only memories of our past that remain with us. These memories become our life, when we can no longer partake in all that we used to do.

Our bones grow weary, our friends disappear, some to other destinations, some leave us for ever to enter the next phase of life where there is peace; maybe meet up with loved ones that have gone before us. Life changes, we change, everything changes! We have now reached our twilight years; life is abandoning us. But let us not dwell on where our life has gone, because we are still here, so let's deal with the knowledge we have gained from our past. Look around: the paintings, the ornaments, the dolls, the photos, they are all our life's treasures. We have held on to them for this very reason. Now we can revisit these special memories, while still sitting in our armchairs.

Each person's treasures are their very own stories. What we see as valuable is unique to us; what one might treasure, another might discard! These are moments that connect the past to the present. If these are taken away before our lives have ended, this is stealing away our lasting memories. We must be allowed to surround ourselves with treasures; this brings comfort and joy into what life we have left.

Moving on

I am not living in the past; I'm living in the now but I am revisiting my past. These beautiful memories, some happy, some sad, but mixed together they are what has taken me on life's journey. They have built me up and let me down at times, but hey ... that's what living is all about, the ups and downs, the roundabouts and roller-coasters. We have all experienced bumpy rides; they make us stronger, which in turn makes us resilient and able to handle all that is thrown at us.

At the time of writing this story most of my energy has been zapped from my body, but hopefully not for ever, rendering it nearly past its use-by date, but my mind is still alive and well. I can't physically visit places I dream about, but that word — dream — can take you to past loves, bring back childhood memories, it can take you wherever you long to visit! To be able to go back and relive the experiences that have moulded my life is simply wonderful. This is the meaning of life ... the period between birth and the present time, all that has been characterised by growth and response. The sole purpose of life is to have lived and enjoyed!

When our twilight years arrive, we must keep our treasures around us to draw upon when all seems lost. Just take a look around, memories will flow back and take you on a journey, whether you go back in time or stay in the present, it doesn't matter, nothing really matters! You can't go forward as ... 'tomorrow is promised to no one'.

My soul mate and I have only recently acted on one of the most important decisions in our life: to downsize from the family home to begin a new life in a retirement village. "Retirement village, but that is for old people, we are not that old?" I tried to convince myself. "That's where you go when you are ready to die, we are a long way from that stage in life, aren't we?" I questioned my soul mate. He was the one who had talked about it for the last couple of years, but I was the one who was young at heart. I still wore modern colourful clothes, not revealing ones, as I knew my body shape had changed, not for the better by any means, but I knew my limitations! Even my hair portrayed my colourful self; it had streaks of red, that was never going to change, well, not in the foreseeable future, this was me ... the one who didn't want to be known as old!

It was not my idea to sell the family home, this was

where I was staying, surrounded by all my treasures until I departed this world to enter my spiritual place. My soul mate, however, had different ideas; he wanted to move to another town. "I need a change, I feel stale, there is nothing left here for me." I could not understand his thinking, of course there was plenty here for him to do, it was just that he wouldn't make the effort to find it. What about the lawns and gardens, he loved to sit and admire the bulbs and flowers as they came out in bloom. How did he think all this happened? Certainly not by itself. Someone had to do the weeding, the pruning, the watering, how else did all this come to fruition? But these chores eluded him, as I was always there to tend to everything; he didn't have a worry in the world. His world was totally different to mine; we seemed to live in different realms. But in writing this, I love whatever realm or kingdom I belonged to, as it makes me happy.

I could see he was tired in his thinking and actions. No wonder he thought he was ready for life in a retirement village, but me ... I certainly was not! He was not a well man and had come close to giving up on life, where as I was still bursting at the seams. When I mentioned the outside of the home needed a new coat of paint, all he could see was money having to be spent ... for what? The house could survive another year in its present state. This got me thinking: if we stayed, was everything going to end in disrepair? Perhaps he was right, was it time to move on? A new challenge, would this give him a new lease of life, is this what he needed? A change of scenery, a new beginning, would this revitalise him? But what of me?

Into the inner workings of the retirement village scene I delved. Brochures arrived from everywhere, so I had plenty of information to take in. We had plans of new villages being built, so I asked my man to pick out a plan he liked and I would do the same. We each picked the one we thought was going to work for us, but this led to disappointment, as we could not agree on one that met both our needs. Of course, my choice was more expensive than my soul mate's, perhaps this is what deterred him from agreeing with me? His thinking was why spend money? It looked better building up in his bank.

Several months had passed, still nothing had been decided. It was talked about nearly every day, but no progress had been made. Something had to happen, as my soul mate was becoming agitated. It was time for action! As there was no sign of his pursuing the matter, I took it upon myself to ring a couple of villages and make an appointment to see what was on offer. So off to Mosgiel we went. This was where my man wanted to go, to be near the city where he could receive the medical treatment he needed, so the choice was left up to him. Location didn't worry me; I was sad, I wasn't ready to be leaving the family home and my arty-farty garden, as this was to be my for-ever home ... not so!

The decision, my soul mate told me, was to make life easier for us both (but his life was easy at our family home). Also, the kids wouldn't have to worry about us in our older age, which was now, according to him.

At the second village we went to, we were made very welcome by a bubbly lady named Shona. As she explained all the details, I could see a frown appearing on my soul mate's face; any mention of spending money brought this on. We roughly knew the ins and outs by now, but he just had to have them reconfirmed. Then he let her know that he found it hard to think of how much money he was going to lose when we departed the village. He hated giving money away; parting with his hard-earned cash was an almost unbearable thought. Good, I thought to myself, he has had a change of heart, we will never be leaving my for-ever home. I was overcome with joy!

The thought of the loss of money did perturb him; he was a businessman, there always had to be a profit, a loss was unacceptable. He mulled over this, but what other choice did he have? I was just recovering from a hip operation so my lawn-mowing days were over for the season, a gardener would have to be employed; this all spelt spending money ... with no return? So, his focus came back to the village scene. When all the benefits were weighed up, it was a no-brainer not to follow up on it. I explained that it wasn't us that would be losing money, it just meant a little less for the kids in the end. Meanwhile we would be living the life of Ned Kelly ... really, this was wishful thinking! Nothing was for nothing any more; it would just mean a less expensive holiday for them, on Mum and Dad's money. Instead of going right around the world on us, they could travel halfway, then they would have to return. Wasn't this worth losing money over, not to have the responsibility or worries of caring for us, their aging parents? This left them free to live their own lives.

Back to our meeting with Shona. She asked us to accompany her in her car and she would take us to have a look at a cottage that had just become available and was ready to occupy. I was recovering from a hip operation and was on crutches. As we walked through the door the sun greeted us with a welcoming smile. Everything was brand spanking new; the cottage had been completely gutted and refitted with all mod cons. As I stood there and looked around, a sudden feeling of belonging overcame me. How could this be happening in just a few short seconds? We were only looking, nothing else? I felt I belonged here, but this was not my home, it was miles away! Had I fallen in love, was this my next home, the one I wanted no part of? As I looked at my soul mate, we smiled at each other; we had found what we were looking for, without so much as a cross word.

Next question was the price. When this was mentioned I cringed, it was more expensive than what we had agreed among ourselves. Suddenly I saw my dream disappearing as soon as it had arrived. Then I heard a voice: "We will take this cottage." Had I heard right? Was this my soul mate's voice, the one who was so money conscious? Had he found a soft moment, was he in fact well? Or was this his dream also being realised, right here in this moment? As I looked around, I became more attracted to it; the patterned cornice, the rose in the lounge ceiling with lovely modern lights, the dining room with macrocarpa tongue-and-groove ceiling, a bay window with a lovely view of the surrounding hills. What was there not to like about this cottage? Nothing; everything was tastefully appointed. I drifted off into fairyland. Was this my new home?

My dream was interrupted with a voice. "I'm sorry, but I have a couple who have made a prior appointment to see this cottage tomorrow, they have first option on it." Did I hear right? Someone else was coming to have a look at our cottage, had they beaten us? No, they couldn't, this was ours, we both had fallen in love with it. Our faces told a sad story, we felt robbed; instead of being happy we were shattered, our dream had been stolen from under our nose! We both sulked all the way back to Alexandra.

That night back in our own home silence reigned. Our minds were numb. We went to bed pinning our dreams on the hope of good news tomorrow. To me, this didn't feel like home any more; everywhere I looked, there was work to be done. At our dream cottage everything was done for us. The lawns were mowed, even the garden could be looked after by the maintenance staff if we didn't want to do it ourselves. How good was that? But my garden was my salvation, so this would come under my care. My soul mate made a suggestion: perhaps he could call Shona and get her to warn the prospective buyers that the trains were very noisy, they would not enjoy living there, but I assured him he couldn't do that ... a good thought though! He was a good thinker, as he had all the time in the world to do this.

The next day the long-awaited phone call came through at lunch time. "Hello, Kelvin, Shona speaking. I have good news, the cottage is yours. The couple were worried about the railway line, so decided to leave it at the moment." Yes, our prayers had been answered. We had found our new home without a quibble from either party. When things are meant to be, they happen without rhyme or reason. Someone from above had looked after us on this occasion; he was definitely on my soul mate's side.

We put down a deposit straight away on the cottage as we had just sold some car parks we owned in Dunedin. Now it was on with the next project ... selling our own home. This brought many tears, as I thought this was my for-ever home! Our next visit to the village was to measure up to see what furniture we needed to bring down and what would have to be sold.

We arrived about mid-afternoon, as we had things to do in the city first. As we drove in, the car park was filled with cars, then I noticed all these walkers parked outside the huge building. Good lord, I thought to myself, what have I let myself in for? But the best was to come! People started emerging from the building in furs and old-fashioned clothes. I could not believe my eyes, "What the hell," I said out loud to my soul mate. "What have we done? This is truly an old person's village, this is not for me. Get me out of here." But it was too late, as we had paid for most of our cottage.

We continued to our cottage; I was in tears. "Fancy ending up living here with all these old people," I sobbed to my soul mate. He felt for me and assured me all would be fine. I didn't even want to get out of the car, but with a lot of coaxing I alighted. As soon as I stepped through the door, my tears dried up as I looked around our new home. The images of all those old people were slowly disappearing, as other things were taking over my mind.

As we were leaving the village, we stopped off at the office to talk to Shona. All the walkers were gone, and the car park had emptied. She greeted us with this: "What a pity you didn't arrive earlier, as we had our midwinter Christmas lunch. The theme was the *Titanic*. You should have seen the residents, they all dressed as passengers on the ship." "Thank you, dear God," I whispered to myself. Now my broken heart was broken no longer; it took on the healing process and again life didn't seem so unbearable.

When I took on board what I had seen and presumed, compared to what I had just been told, my nightmare turned to hilarity. Even to this day I will never forget that day when my world nearly came to an end. There is an up-side to this story, as now I am one of those fragile-looking people I dared to think were on their last legs.

Please forgive me, dear residents, you are my family and hopefully we can laugh about this for many years to come. Who on earth did I think I was? To answer truthfully, I thought I was too young to be part of this village. I had not faced the truth as to my age, but now I have reconciled with myself, please let us call a truce?

Our new beginning

We are now settled in our dream cottage in our retirement village and loving every moment. Several kind neighbours welcomed us with baking, which we thought was a lovely gesture, especially as we were complete strangers. This made us feel we were being accepted into our new community. I look back and wonder why I was so against moving in the first place. Was it because I hadn't got my head around the fact that I was now in my seventies, I was a pensioner along with all the other village people? But I am still a young seventy ... if there is such a thing?

I am now reunited with most of my treasures, even though only a small portion of my stones were transported down by reluctant family members. But special thanks went to an understanding sibling who stored my left-over stones in his garage, away from prying eyes. "You have enough here already, you don't need any more," my soul mate sternly told me. But he was wrong ... I did need them, now they are back where they belong ... in my garden, much to his disgust! Men don't seem to share the same sentiments towards important things, such as stones, they are not like us females. But then, women are from Venus and men are from Mars, so of course we are different, in fact many light years apart!

The weather has taken a turn for the worst today, it is crying bucketfuls of water, even the sun has decided not to venture out. No sense in coming out, only to get wet. I nestle into my recliner and there in front of me, paintings adorn our walls. I suppose you would call us collectors of art and other bits and pieces, all treasures of course! Each painting harbours a story of its own.

My favourite, a painting by an Italian artist called Pino Daeni, fills me with joy each time my eyes make contact with it. There, half perched on a table in a study, is the maid in her white pinny; she looks exhausted, pieces of her hair have fallen untidily from her topknot. Perhaps she has stopped for a minute to have a well-earned rest, while serving the evening meal or a dinner party? But what catches the eye is the way the artist has captured the light as it reflects off her white pinny across the tablecloth. One wonders if she is an Italian or perhaps a French maid, but that's not important; what is important, she has a quiet calm about her that draws one in.

Pino Daeni is a well-known Italian painter. His subjects are mainly women and children, this for a very good reason. He lived in a little Italian village and when war broke out, he was too young to go and fight for his country. All the menfolk that were of age left, so he was in charge of the womenfolk; he had to help them fill their pails with water from the village well, along with other male duties. To help pass the days, he would sketch the women and young girls as they went about their chores, and later he would turn his sketches into paintings. These were the subjects before him; thus, this theme formed his career as an artist. His paintings capture the very essence of femininity.

The night before the art auction, art was put out to be viewed. We both settled for a Pino Daeni painting, portraying a mother and her two children on the beach, but this all changed on auction night when a new painting was unveiled and put on view. There it was, *Evening*

Thoughts. I instantly felt a connection to this painting; it made me feel warm inside, so now it was going to be mine! We forgot about the lady on the beach and brought this lovely painting. This is the one hanging on the wall before me, the one that I love to this very day. Gosh, where had the afternoon gone? I had revisited my past. If I didn't have this treasure, I could not have filled in a nostalgic afternoon. At the time of the auction we were cruising on the high seas, probably sailing into Hong Kong.

The rain has not eased today, it still insists on soaking everyone's gardens and more! In general, it is proving to be a 'pain in the butt'. No gardening again today. Probably time to remove some dust from my furniture, this I have been putting off for some time, but not for a minute longer. Yes, the polishing rags need to come out and commence work. As I worked away, I come to my favourite piece of wooden art. To polish it is a pleasure! This is a beautiful carved figure of a naked woman; it is eye-catching to say the least, but I am not embarrassed to have it on display in my lounge as it is a masterpiece. I remember when we bought this treasure from a talented woodcarver named Rob. He was a background sort of person, but his talent as a carver was to be admired. He was commissioned to sculpt this figure for a wealthy American, which took him four months to finish, then he shipped it to America. Days later he received a phone call from the buyer saying he was returning it, as he was not happy with the darker wood around the neck area. This is not unusual when working with a natural product. Rob was out of pocket over this as he stood the shipping costs. It was a commissioned work gone pear-shaped, which he took to heart, through no fault of his own.

Then I came on to the scene and instantly fell in love with this piece of art. It was one of my many 'have to have' moments. Rob did not charge me the price that the American was going to pay, for which I was thankful, but it still cost $2,500 and worth every penny! I think he was glad to see it leave his workshop, as it held bad memories. My soul mate did, however, donate to him some flitches of timber he had brought back from the West Coast. This he was grateful for, as he could carve more treasures for someone else, so both parties were happy. I was ecstatic! Sadly, only a couple of years later Rob passed away at a young age, so this figure reminds me of this talented young man. Life can be unpredictable; it does not choose who should leave, or when!

Taking treasures away

Great! The sun has chased the rain away, but I have to admit everything looks refreshed and happy, so we must give the rain some accolades. If only it would let us know when it was going to appear, not just surprise us, instead make an appointment, but in reality, that is not how life works! Nothing is on order; acceptance is the name of the game and one must learn to deal with whatever comes their way. As I have learnt, and so has everyone else, life was not designed to be a walk in the park. Imagine if we received all we desired, we would be happy for a short while perhaps, then what? Boredom would set in and the feeling of appreciation would vanish, what ungrateful creatures we would become. To achieve one's own personal triumphs throughout life, the wanting, the waiting, the saving to buy that special thing, that's when we really appreciate the very essence of life. It wasn't given to us, we earned it ourselves, this is called self-satisfaction! To be looked after from the cradle to the grave has its down-sides. Having everything handed to you on a platter just isn't satisfying; we need to own our own success.

For me, having my own treasures keeps my mind focused and occupied. Twice I have witnessed elderly people who have lost their partners and been talked into moving in with family. At first, this seems a kind gesture, but here is an example of what can happen. The son-in-law went to his father-in-law's home to help sort out what he was allowed to bring with him to his new home. The elderly man didn't have a lot, but his dearest possessions were a box of letters. This was his lifeline; he could take them out and read them and be transported back to the days he had met these people and what had transpired from these meetings. In other words, they were his treasures. The son-in-law looked inside the box and decided it was rubbish, it was not coming into his home, so without his father-in-law's say, he emptied the contents into the drum in the backyard and set it alight. Tears flowed from the elderly man's eyes as he watched his life memories leave this earth in a puff of black smoke. Now his past was gone, this was the beginning of the end!

He was an insurance agent during the building of the Roxburgh dam. Having the insight to teach himself the Dutch language allowed him to sell his company's policy to the new immigrants, who flocked to this man who could speak in their tongue. He made many friends and they showed their appreciation by corresponding with him over many years. Thus, the box of letters, his treasures, the ones that were gone for ever. His past was destroyed and he felt sad and empty.

Having moved in with his daughter and son-in-law he felt lonely as they both worked, so he was left in the house on his own day after day. He knew no one at his new address. He would sit and look around the room trying to find something that would bring a little joy, but there was nothing that let him revisit his past. Everything surrounding him belonged to someone else, they were their treasures, they meant nothing to him. Day after day the tears flowed; why was he here? If only he had his letters, at least he could take them out and read them, then he could connect with the writer, bringing a little happiness to his heart. Emptiness filled his soul and he became depressed. 'Why am I still here?' he asked himself many times. He begged to be taken each night as he lay in his bed, he had nothing to look forward to, only more lonely days. His soul was destroyed, his memory dimmed then started to fade, he was lost to a world of darkness. This was his existence for another six months, then one day, by the grace of God, he was taken from this life to his long-awaited peace.

Family can have good intentions, but are they right for the one left? No one should be on their own, everyone needs company, especially elderly people. This is the single best thing about living in a village environment: one is never lonely, someone is always near to call upon, or just to say hello to. I know when we shifted, our children had their say in what we should and shouldn't take to our new home, but these helpful hints were blissfully ignored. We didn't need our children's opinions; we were of sound mind ... well, we thought we were ... obviously they had their doubts!

My beloved stones

As we grow older, it is time to disinherit our children; we housed them, fed them and pampered to most of their requests. Now was the time to drop the guilt and live in our own twilight zone. Our children's lives became their own. They make their own choices, some were not our cup of tea, but who are we to judge? We don't know everything, in fact we made silly decisions at times, but that is all part and parcel of life. Our children even tried offering us advice at times ... excuse me ... who had experienced life and who were just beginning? This deserved a laugh!

We often joked about the advice given to us, when they wouldn't listen to what we tried to tell them. They didn't need advice, they knew it all, they were worldly, we were old. We both felt we didn't want to be a burden on our children, but to be totally honest, neither of us could have lived with any of them, so the retirement village was the best option. Also, my soul mate wanted me to be in a safe environment in case his health worsened and I was left on my own. My thoughts on village life were different then to what they are now! I felt I was too young (at heart) but on writing this, there is nowhere else I would rather be. I love it here, this is my safe haven.

We try to have a walk most days and although the cottages all look the same, the gardens are so different as each resident adds their flavour to their patch. Everything is kept neat and tidy; nothing is allowed to look unkempt. Just along from us by someone's letterbox a lonely frog sits on a seat with a lovely red rose in his hand. Above him is a sign 'Waiting' but no one has turned up yet. Sadly, as the weeks go by, still he sits alone, so I am hoping perseverance will pay off one day soon. If not, I might just be forced into lending a helping hand and find him a mate. A man can only wait so long! I don't want to find him gone one day to seek companionship elsewhere, as he makes me smile. He is my daily dose of happiness.

Today I am spending in the garden. My herbs and lettuces are looking great, they are sprinting away. I have adjusted some of my favourite stones; I regularly move them around, this doesn't surprise them, as they are used to being moved. They never get a chance to get bored with their neighbours, as they are never in the same place long enough to become familiar with each other. I have fun trying new places for them, to show them off to their best advantage, and mine!

I love stones, they cost zilch and one gets to spend time on beaches and river beds when collecting them. Out in the fresh air, in the wide-open spaces, what could be more invigorating? One of my favourites — I say one because I have many — are the pink ones I picked up from a tidal beach at Granity on the West Coast. As per expected on the Coast, it was drizzling the day we visited, so my soul mate elected to stay in the vehicle; he wasn't going to get wet collecting stones, they weren't worth the hassle. But drizzle didn't deter me, I was into it with my buckets, looking for the round and oval-shaped ones. Never before had I seen stones this colour. I have since discovered during my searches that certain stones are peculiar to certain areas. Having filled my buckets, I struggled back to the vehicle and lifted them into the boot, then we made our way across the road to a little hotel to get a bite to eat. I had worked up an appetite that had to be satisfied.

It was a typical out-of-the-way drinking place; a dog lay asleep on the carpet beside the bar. He had had his fill and was sleeping it off! The barman yelled instructions to someone in the background to whip up a couple of sandwiches for some hungry travellers ... this being us, of course. To be social I ordered a wine for myself and a raspberry and Coke for my soul mate. The barman or owner tried to extract from us what we were doing in his patch. I could hardly tell him we were stealing stones off his beach; perhaps he was a greenie and would take offence, thus not deliver our sandwiches, which we needed as we were famished. I thought quickly and offered him a quick exclamation: "We are on our way to Karamea." Why did I say this? It wasn't true.

Out came our lunch, two huge Dagwood sandwiches bursting at the seams. How on earth were we meant to eat these, all the ingredients were hanging out the sides? This would not be acceptable in a Michelin kitchen, but this was typical of a West Coast snack, big and bountiful and slapped together, it was the norm. There was very little finesse but we forgave them for this, as they tasted yummy. This time I didn't eat with my eyes! Once we were finished and our bellies were fed, we thanked the barman and left his premises. My soul mate started the vehicle and we headed off in the direction we had come. As I looked back, the barman was waving his arms frantically, trying to tell us we were heading in the wrong direction, this was not the way to Karamea. My little white lie had caught me out, so we pretended not to see him and kept on driving. The stones were rattling away in the boot, perhaps in protest for having been stolen and taken from their familiar surroundings! But they would be cared for in their new home, there was no fear of that. They had now become members of a stone lover's collection!

We drove for several hours before stopping at a little picnic area, just north of Greymouth. It was right by the sea and we could see and hear the waves crashing onto the beach. A little stream had made its way down from the hills, through a culvert that ran beneath the road, until it emerged with the sea. I walked down by the stream and was totally delighted to see these beautiful egg-shaped grey stones with flecks of mica shining through them. I looked to see where they might have come from and noticed huge hills in the background. This must have been where their journey began. As they dislodged and tumbled their way down the hilly terrain, this caused the churning that smoothed and shape them to look like eggs. I called for my soul mate to come and have a look, which he obeyed without so much as a grumble, and, like me, he was in total awe of the uniform shape of the stones. It was only then we noticed the waves were getting too close for comfort, so we hightailed it out of there. This would be tomorrow's mission, to come back and do some more gathering. I loved it when my soul mate saw the pleasure I got from searching the landscape for things that took my eye. Mind you, I was the daydreamer from Venus, he was just a plain, sensible unmoved male from Mars!

Here we are today, back at my secret place. The tide was out, so we had sole charge of our piece of paradise. Out came the bags; we were relegated to bags as the two buckets we had intended to fill were already overflowing. The gathering commenced! It didn't take us long to fill our bags as every stone was a uniform shape, it was unbelievable. Even my soul mate was turned on by this discovery — sorry, wrong expression, I should have said excited by this discovery. Stones certainly didn't turn him on, it took something a little more feminine to have this effect on him. Once the bags were filled, we carried them to the vehicle and put them in the boot with their cousins from Granity. I was ecstatic with my finds; they would accompany me home and be displayed in my arty-farty garden.

The following day as we drove up the West Coast highway towards Haast. I knew there was one more stop to make; this was at a little settlement called Bruce Bay. This area was well known for its pure-white stones. I knew all about this place as I had been here many times before for this specific task, and here we were today, for the very same reason. But as we entered the little settlement, I noticed that things had changed. Where was the accessible beach, what was that building partly obscured by the bushes doing there? That was new. Then I saw the sign, it was a marae, how did it get there? As we pulled over, we were greeted by a rock groin. What had happened to the little bank that I used to jump down to get to the beach? What was once an accessible area was now a non-accessible one!

I climbed from the vehicle and tried to get my bearings; everything had changed, it was not the lovely place as I remembered it. I walked over to the groin and there below in the sand lay my pure-white stones begging me to come and take them home with me. How was I going to get to them? It would mean clambering down the rocks, which would prove a bit of a mission. Was this to stop us stone thieves from taking stones from the beach? Did the building of the marae dictate that these beautiful stones now belonged to Maori?

My soul mate wouldn't venture out of the vehicle; he was staying put, he wasn't going to risk his life for a bag of stones! But, me on the other hand would risk life and limb to get to those stones. With much difficulty I navigated my way down the rock groin, thinking all the way, thank goodness my soul mate didn't make the journey. I could just imagine the colourful words that would have escaped his lips, putting a damper on my excitement.

I was happy to be gathering them on my own, it was peaceful as I only chose my special-shaped ones. If he was with me, as long as the bags got filled with whatever-shaped stones, the sooner the better, as then we would be on our way home. I was yelled at several times and told not to be so bloody fussy, this call came from the man from Mars, sitting in the comfort of the vehicle. How dare he speak to the lady from Venus in such a manner, but then I remembered, we were many light years apart ... thus the outburst, he knew no different. What did they teach them up there?

My stones were on their way back to the family home

where they would have pride of place and I could enjoy them and remember all the drama they caused … none of it called for, of course! Not for a minute did I think another shift was in store for them, or myself. Never in a hundred years! This was my for-ever home, but no, this was not to be.

They are now rehoused in my village garden. I had to beg family members, who along with their father thought I was mad, wanting to take rubbishy old stones to my new abode. But they didn't understand, I loved my stones, they were part of me! If it wasn't for an understanding sibling who brought them down, three loads in all, I would never have seen them again. Thank you, dear brother. They are a story on their own, my story, one I like to share. People admire them, all except the man from Mars; deep down he probably likes them a little bit, but won't allow himself to outwardly display his emotions, not over something as petty as stones!

Life goes on

Today is Sunday, normally a quiet day at the village, but not today. A special show has been arranged for the residents, so this is where we are. It is a country and western session, so we will all merrily sing along and enjoy ourselves. It is lovely to see so many residents coming out and supporting the entertainment. The bar is open so most are participating in a little tipple! The great thing about village entertainment, we can all walk to the Residents Club and not have to worry about getting a ticket from the appropriate authorities for indulging in a little pleasure. Another big plus for village lifestyle.

After putting together an easy tea we retire to our lounge. The two glasses of wine I consumed had worked their magic, relaxation had taken over and it wasn't long before I was entering on another journey, revisiting my past. It was that painting, the portrait of the girl with the saddest eyes one could ever imagine. It was certainly a tear-jerker, there was anguish in those eyes; where did it come from, had the artist suffered? This is what drew me to this painting, and it wasn't until all was explained, that I was prompted to bid for it at the auction, even if it was just to remind me what was behind those piercing eyes.

The artist's name was Martiros Manoukian. His life began in Armenia, before he moved with his family to Russia as a young boy. He became firmly established in Russian art history and was regarded as one of their greatest artists. But despite his popularity, he was frequently arrested by the KGB, who considered his art was becoming too Westernised. He longed to leave Russia and settle in America, where he could paint freely, but it took him seven years to obtain the final approval from Russian authorities. The night before he left, the KGB visited him and took a hammer to his hands breaking several fingers, thus hoping he would never paint again.

My painting is called *Ethereal Whisper* ('ethereal' meaning of the region above the clouds; very delicate) and was painted after this terrible happening. All his drama was portrayed in the girl's eyes; I loved this story, it tore at my heart. Every time I look at this painting, I think of Martiros Manoukian and remember his suffering, for what? For freedom to paint what was in his heart. I thank my lucky stars that I wasn't born in a country that dictated what I could and couldn't do. Freedom … a word without a price! A word of unlimited access to whatever, one many of us in the Western world take for granted.

This was another piece of art we bought while on the cruise ship, sailing our way to Japan for the Cherry Blossom Festival. Each day we went to the art auctions and picked out what took our eye, ready to outbid other interested parties. Some we missed out to higher bidders, but thank goodness for this, otherwise we would have gone into bankruptcy by the end of the cruise. What good would the paintings be then, if I didn't have a home to house them?

Art my passion

I have some paintings of my own displayed on our cottage walls. In the old family home (past tense) they were relegated to the long hallway, to make room for the more prominent, or should I say, more famous works of art. Mine I thought were too inferior to be displayed in the public eye. But I had a change of heart when we moved into the village; this was a new beginning, if you could call it that, as we were nearing the tail end of our lives, to be quite honest! It was time for me to hang a couple of my favourite paintings in our dining room, where I could see them and enjoy my personal creations. This was a piece of me, reminding me when I embarked onto the art scene. I never became famous, but I did manage to sell a number of pieces at art exhibitions.

In fact, I did feel famous for one moment in my life, when I entered a painting in an art exhibition in Queenstown. The night before the official opening, all the local dignitaries along with the artists were invited to a special showing. I felt so proud, there was my masterpiece hanging on the wall in front of all these important people! We were all mixing together over drinks and nibbles when my soul mate wondered off, but minutes later he was back. "What does it mean when there is a red dot on a painting?" he asked. I told him it meant it was sold. "Well, you have just sold yours, congratulations." I was ecstatic; we had only been here for less than half an hour and my painting was sold. But I had put a large price on it, seeing this was Queenstown. This was the moment when I felt famous! Later in the night the organiser brought the buyer to meet me. He was a local Queenstown man and he told me he loved my painting. This was a big moment for me, I felt so proud.

The exhibition ran for a fortnight, so any paintings that were sold had to remain on show for the entire two weeks. This meant my painting would be on display, for visitors to admire, for this length of time. How pleasing! One day, a lady from the exhibition rang me to say she had been approached by an American lady who wanted to buy my painting. She was so persistent that the art organiser contacted the man who had purchased it to see if he would on-sell it. The American buyer offered him twice my asking price, but he refused. I was then asked if I would be interested in doing a commissioned work for her and then send it off to America? She wanted an exact replica of the existing painting. I thought about it, then my mind went back to Rob's nude sculpture and how the American buyer refused to pay for it and how costly it was for him. Would this be any different? I asked myself. I decided not to follow up on this, as one can never do an exact replica, because painting is a mood thing. To try to recapture that moment in time when I painted my masterpiece would be nigh on possible. So, my fame was short-lived! It was but a moment in time! The lady in charge of the exhibition wrote me a note to say she could have sold my painting six times over, as people loved it. In fact, when I finished painting it, my soul mate didn't want me to sell it, as it was his favourite. Not for one moment did I think it would sell in Queenstown! I thought it would be coming home with us in the back seat of the car after the exhibition had ended. How mistaken can one be?

All my life I have admired art. I loved visiting exhibitions, not thinking for one moment I would choose to paint one day. It wasn't until I retired that I ventured onto the art scene. One day I went and brought some acrylic paints and a couple of canvases. I loved oils, but they were the *crème de la crème* of media; that would come later, much later, I told myself. My soul mate thought I was very ambitious, as he pointed out to me that I had trouble drawing a straight line, how was I going to paint? This did nothing to boost my confidence; I tried not to let it bother me! But to his and my amazement, the end result of my first painting was quite remarkable. He was totally amazed at my first attempt, who knew what the future held?

True to form, I did graduate to oils and loved this medium. I enjoyed mixing the colours, but most satisfying was the thickness one could apply the oils. It gave the paintings depth. They took a lot longer to dry, so if changes had to be made this was possible, even the next day. It was a forgiving medium. I signed up for a weekend workshop with an artist named Randall Froude, who lived at Kimbell, a little community this side of Fairlie. His lessons were invaluable; he taught us how to anchor stones under water so they didn't look like they were floating, also the secret to painting water to give it depth. The sky was another object he focused on. I loved all I learnt at his workshop. When my soul mate came to picked me up, he allowed me to buy one of Randall's paintings. I was thrilled. I chose a painting of a pink rose and two buds; it was framed in a wide gold frame, making it look like it was an antique piece of art.

Thus, my decision to put some of my artwork on display. Why hide it away, when it is a gift to be able to put your thoughts on canvas and be proud of your achievements? To paint, one must be in a peaceful place in one's own mind. It is not something you can plan. The best paintings evolve when in a tranquil space with no distractions and no time restrictions. There only needs to be you in your world, a world where nothing else is relevant. This is the perfect environment to paint.

Sadly, I no longer paint. I have sold all my painting gear, that era has gone. Our lives dived into darkness for four years and my peace was not able to be found again, thus bringing my painting days to an end. But I have my memories before me, reminding me of those wonderful times when I achieved beyond my wildest dreams, when I almost made it to the elite status! Not really, I'm not into elite. Thankfully I took photos of all my paintings and have them in a book of memories. I have recorded for what price I sold them and who purchased them, but for a couple of exceptions, when they were sold through an art gallery.

Battle scars!

Tonight, at bedtime I feel wide awake. This usually means a story is conjuring up in my mind and needs to be released. My soul mate is snuggled up in bed, but for me, I'm far from tired. Perhaps if I have a hot shower, this will make me sleepy, then I can join him.

Here I am standing under the shower with the hot water cascading over my body, when suddenly my eyes capture all my battle scars. How did they get there? I asked myself. This body had caused me so much embarrassment over the years. I feel ashamed when I think back to my teenage years, when all was taunt and my body parts were in their rightful places. But over the years, muffins have appeared. I learnt this term from the younger generation; I always thought muffins were things you ate, but apparently not! I had only ever known them as fat rolls, but must admit muffins describe them in a more lovable manner. But today that shame has gone as I am at peace with myself. My body has a lot of history with it; those battle scars were all caused by family members, none of them was my fault. Isn't it sad to think these wounds were all other people's doing? The appropriate people should have been be held accountable.

Number one scar was caused by my eldest son. He decided to make my life difficult right from the start, so decided on a caesarean birth. This meant he could just lie there and be lifted out, leaving me the one scarred for life! Three years later my second son decided he was not going to be outdone, so chose the same option as his older brother. He didn't want to struggle into this world, when he could leisurely lie there and wait to be lifted out; this was the easy option for him. No pain to him ... all to me! More scarring!

Four years later I was advised by my doctor to have my tubes tied because of complications. "It's a simple procedure, keyhole surgery is all that is required." Then he hesitated: "Oh no, we can't do that, you have caesarean scars therefore it will require surgery." Did I hear right, surely not another scar? "What about your husband? There is a new procedure out for men called a vasectomy. All it requires is a simple snip. Tell him to come and see me and I will write out a referral letter and he can go and get it done. This will save you from having another operation." What a wonderful idea: instead of me suffering, all he needed was a little 'snip', not even he would see where this procedure had taken place. It was less invasive for him, he would have no scars, all he would have was a story to tell ... if he dared!

I rushed home in a jubilant state; great, I was spared from another scar, how wonderful. I picked my moment to discuss this prickly situation with my soul mate. But if he loved me then I could see no problems. When I asked him, he was not impressed, he was a man, men didn't have these sorts of things done to them, this was women's stuff. This proved to me one of two things: his manly pride would be hurt or he was chickening out because he was afraid?

As the weeks went by, every now and again I would bring this sensitive subject to light, but to no avail. In the end I had to take drastic measures, so gave him the ultimatum: sex or no sex. This made him sit up and take notice, so of course he chose sex, but what man wouldn't, so it was off to see the doctor. He came home with the referral letter and went to the bedroom and put it in his top draw next to his undies. I thought what a great place for the letter, every time he went to get clean undies it would remind him of his obligation to me. Sadly, it did not! Was this too much to hope for?

One fine day several weeks later a new play came to light. My soul mate's deaf friend pulled up at the end of our driveway, then climbed out of his car. As he made his way towards our house, I wondered what was wrong with him, as his legs were very bandy and he seemed to have trouble walking. I thought he was being silly so called my man over to have a look. We both burst out laughing as he finally reached our door. Next thing he was flinging his arms around yelling in his mumbo-jumbo language. I fetched a chair for him to be seated, as he seemed excited about something. All I could make sense of was "No, no, sore" and he was pointing to his groin area. "What is he doing that for?" I asked my soul mate. Then, when he explained what all the ruckus was about, I didn't know whether to laugh or cry. He had had a vasectomy several days earlier and was still in terrible pain. Surely not, this couldn't be right, the doctor said it was a 'simple snip'. The first words that came out of my mouth were these: "Perhaps this happened to him because he is deaf." How bloody stupid of me, but I didn't want my man to be put off by all this.

After this visit I was too frightened to mention the word 'vasectomy' again, I had to let things cool down for a while. I wanted my soul mate to forget this ever happened to his friend. But strangely enough several of my girlfriends' husbands had had it done with no side effects. It was becoming a bit of a fashion statement among the men. Hopefully my man was going to partake in the latest fashion?

One day as I was putting clean undies in my soul mate's drawer, I noticed the letter had disappeared. I smiled to myself, he had finally decided to have it done; see, perseverance had paid off in the end. I knew I could trust him with this decision, he was thinking of me after all ... or was he? That night as I was emptying the rubbish bin, there was the letter, torn to shreds. I then knew what was in store for me: another scar!

My next two scars, impressive as they are, matched each other perfectly, one on each side of my thighs. These were my mother's fault. She had passed her arthritic genes on to me, hence two hip replacements. Since writing this, I found a little saying so thought I would slip it in before going to print: 'Don't be a victim of your genes'. But I am a victim, I have just explained why.

As I first mentioned, through no fault of my own were any of these battle scars of my own doing! All I can add is thank goodness I wasn't born in the Stone Age, otherwise my scars would have been on display for the whole village to see. In modern today, clothes hide a multitude of sins, thank God. No wonder I love clothes so much. But wait a minute, a thought has just come to me: if I was born in the Stone Age, no one would have seen my scars, because I wouldn't have had any ... I would probably have died in childbirth!

I have learnt not to be ashamed of my body, it is the way it is! This is me. I am still here enjoying life, only I know what lies beneath the outer layer, thank God. Ladies, rejoice! My goodness, half the night has disappeared and it is now early morning, but it has been worth every minute, to put pen to paper and share my secrets with you. This is not what I expected was coming when I felt the urge to write, but I have learnt that sometimes our actions can surprise us. My soul mate knows nothing about being in my story, but really, he is the star, although he didn't play out the main role; he reneged, so his stardom was short-lived! My man was no longer my hero; he has been relegated and now has become my timid pussycat!

Don't let age stop you

My new age, or should I say my old age, indulgence is writing. I never knew I could put a story together, but once again I proved myself wrong! It never ceases to amaze me how often one can surprise oneself. I started writing verse because it was fun, not a lot of concentration was needed, just imagination and I seem to have plenty of that! I started by watching the clouds floating by, then I decided to catch one and float on high. See, there it was already, imagination, it will take you wherever you wish to visit. See how easy it is, no university education is needed, just relax, it is a magical world out there waiting to be explored. If I can do it, so can you. I printed my quirky little verses and put them into books. I learnt off the internet how to bind my own books, so am really proud of myself. I open them when I need a little cheering up; they make me laugh. How could I have written such rubbish, but happy rubbish?

Next, I graduated to family trees. This was a lot more intense; it required a lot of research and a good memory for dates and names, neither of which was my strong point! But one year on, I had solved all the mysteries that surrounded my mother's background. Sadly, she knew very little about her ancestors, and by this time she had passed away. I visited her graveside regularly, letting her know what I had discovered. I hoped my dad was listening, as he always thought his family were a little above Mum's. His father was of middle class, he was a tailor and made suits for businessmen; Mum's father was of working class, he was a flax cutter during the depression. But my mother's family history far exceeded what we could have imagined. I even published a book called *de Marisco*, which covers my mother's background right back to 1066, to the Battle of Hastings era. Her colourful history awakened my thirst to delve into history which took me down many new pathways. Many of my *de Marisco* books have sold worldwide as more and more people are searching their family histories. As soon as they enter the words 'de Marisco', the computer automatically brings up my book, so I am still receiving royalties from Amazon. Dad's history was ordinary in comparison, so I let him down gently, I didn't want to hurt him. I was a dad's girl, inheriting his gentle ways and his sense of humour. But Mum, you were the star!

After the family trees were completed, what next? I had caught the writing bug and just wanted to keep going. It became my first love; my soul mate was relegated to second place. There was something annoying me in the back of my mind. I wanted to write about it, but I knew there would be consequences if it wasn't handled properly. It had put our lives on hold for four years. I felt it was now time to put pen to paper and get it out. I hired a digital publisher from Auckland to help me with what I could and couldn't write, without a libel case against me.

We went through my dilemma with a fine-tooth comb, until it became libel free. I mixed reality with fiction, changed names and places, anything that could connect the actual person to the story. The story was still true but disguised. But if the person the story pertained to read it, she would recognise herself immediately, as there couldn't be two people so wicked living on this planet? Without positive proof it would only be her word against mine, but as I have learnt, to go head to head with a person who doesn't know the truth from a lie, you become the loser! But I will take my chances!

It was time for me to begin my writing career, my story could now be told. Thus, the start of my first novel. Little did I realise for my story to become a novel it had to contain sixty thousand words. Away I went; I had a book written in my mind before I even started, I had so much to write. When I finished my story several weeks later, I could not believe that only had ten thousand words had registered on my word count. Where had the rest gone? The counter was obviously faulty. I read it through and to my annoyance it was telling the truth. What was I going to do now? It had to grow another fifty thousand words. Where to from here? I was still upset even after having released all my feelings. Only one more thing to do: turn my target into an even more evil person. The more I thought about this, the more worked up I became.

Off I went into the world of fiction. It was fun, nothing had to be true any more, I became the main character. I've never been this sort of person in real life, but believe me, in fiction miracles can happen. I had turned into a bad person, in fact a real bitch, causing trouble wherever I went. The days came and went, every spare minute was spent with my pen and paper. Then it had to be transferred to my computer, until one day I looked at the word count and it had reached sixty-one thousand, five hundred words. I had done it! My novel was finished, I rejoiced, it was easy ... not true! Thus, my first novel: I called it *Isobella*.

One can get caught up in the story, even become the heroine falling in love with the man of her dreams. It is an escape from everyday life. We can dream and become whoever, the choice is ours, and as we grow older, we still have feelings that can be brought to life by reading a book of our choice, be it romance, fiction, historical or a biography. There is something out there for everyone. This is why I love writing. A lot of my writing holds pieces of my life mixed with fiction, consequently nobody but myself knows what is true and what is false. To remain anonymous gives the story a certain mystique. To a reader it is just another story, to the author it is a disguise. Where else can one carry out their fantasies other than in a book? No one is hurt by this.

I have since written another six novels and four books and am happiest when I have a pen in my hand; I feel lost without it. My latest novel is a realistic fiction, meaning it is based on real facts mixed with fiction. Due to the nature of the story, for fear of retaliation, I had to be careful not to put myself in a position of being unsafe. There are always people out there waiting for loopholes so they can make easy money, as I have experienced in real life! I just have to hope the 'ideas' jar does not become empty!

Beware of scammers!

While on the computer one night my eye caught a commercial being endorsed by Mike Hosking. I like Mike, he is a straight shooter, he shoots from the hip, not worrying what people think of him or his actions. He does his homework and tells the facts as they are, like it or not! I stopped on this page, as it told how he had made his wealth, and he wanted to share his good fortune with others. Not at all like the Mike that I thought he was, but perhaps he had had a change of heart and become Mr Nice Guy? I read it through several times trying to take it all in. I am no slouch when it comes to life, well, I didn't think I was. I was convinced it was genuine, simply because Mike had endorsed it. I called to my soul mate to come and have a look. The subject was the 'Bitcoin', which we had heard about, but did not fully understand how it worked. But because it was endorsed by a highflyer, then it must be okay? I was too clever to be caught up in a scam.

We talked about it and decided to invest one thousand dollars for a start. I went ahead and filled out the relevant details required; phone numbers and how much we were going to invest. Later that night I received a phone call from a guy named Max about our interest in Bitcoin. We had an interesting conversation; he was very polite and asked me what age bracket I was in. I let him know that I was retired. He asked me to put my money I wanted to invest into his bank account. This I did, and he said he would ring back as soon as it had gone through.

Half an hour later when Max rang, he told me the credit card had been declined. I couldn't understand this, as I knew there were sufficient funds in that account to meet the payment, so I let him know this. He assured me it didn't say insufficient funds, so he knew that wasn't the problem. He asked me to put it through again, in case I had put in a wrong pin number. This I did with my soul mate's approval. Not long after, the phone went again: "Hello, Margaret, that payment has been declined again. Will you ring the bank and tell them, you have approved this payment to go through? It was after bank hours, so I looked up their after-hours number and made a call. A man answered, and I asked him why they had declined my payment. He asked me for my details, then told me to hold the line while he investigated. He came back with an answer: "We have stopped this payment as this is a scam.

You are not the first person we have blocked payments for, these are scammers hard at work." I told him that Mike Hosking had endorsed the Bitcoin, and that was why we followed it up. He explained that the scammers were using high-profile names without the people's consent. I was shocked. I thanked him for his co-operation and for saving our one thousand dollars. I felt sick ... I was conned.

I thought that was the end, but the phone rang again. It was Max, and before he had time to speak, I unleashed my frustrations in a very unladylike manner, telling him he was a low-life, fancy scamming the elderly. "No, Margaret, the bank has refused you simply because they don't want you taking your money out of their bank and depositing it elsewhere. It is your money; you can tell them what you want to do with it. Ring them back and demand that you have authorised this payment." His sheer persistence annoyed me, along with his lies, so I told him to 'bugger off' and not to contact me again, then hung up in his ear.

Two months have passed and we are still being woken at all hours of the night by this con man, who seems to have no idea what time it is in New Zealand. My soul mate has used unholy language towards him, but he is not put off! I felt so stupid, here was this modern, up-to-date, computer-savvy woman who thought she was too smart to be scammed, but the scammers had outsmarted her. Well, not really, because they never got our money, but they did dent my pride badly! Since all this has happened Mike Hosking has announced that scammers are using high-profile names to feather their own nest, to be aware, not to be taken in by them. I have learnt by experience, it doesn't matter how clever you think you are, the scammers are always one step ahead. I won't be deviating from my mindset ever again; once bitten, twice shy ... were these my famous last words?

Syria's woes!

I love reading about world affairs so wait patiently each week for the 'World Focus', a supplement that arrives with Monday's *Otago Daily Times*. I was saddened reading and listening to all the horrible things happening overseas, especially in Syria, where so many women and children are displaced. My heart goes out to these innocent people. I asked myself, who are these terrorists, the Taliban and the jihadists, and what part did the Kurds have to play in all this? I didn't really understand who were friends and who were foe. So, my trusty computer and I decided to undertake to find out who these people were, and why they had become terrorists. Night after night we band together to find why these young men destroyed their lives and others ... and for what? Once I acquired a little understanding, it all started to come together.

This led me deeper into uncharted territory; next came the question, which countries had nuclear weapons and hydrogen bombs? This information blew me away; was our world that volatile? We are not living in a peaceful environment any more, that has been taken away from us.

Back to the jihadists, my burning question was, why were they killing so many people in France and Belgium and around the world? I was fascinated by what I discovered; suddenly life became a bit more real! A lot of these young men were French citizens born in France to Muslim parents. As they grew into young adults, no one would employ them because of their ethnicity, therefore they had no purpose in life. They couldn't marry as they had no money to support a wife and children, their lives were virtually worthless. These young men were being recruited through the internet by jihad terrorists, they were promised they would become heroes by sacrificing their lives for Allah. A pang of sorrow filled my heart, I felt for these young men. What would life be like for them, no work, no income, no hope and no future?

Not long after I had discovered this, in the newspaper appeared this quote from the Pope: 'These young men need employment, please give them work so that their lives are meaningful. Without a future there is no hope or no joy in their lives. Every young person deserves a future; it is their right.' I thought these were words of wisdom from such a powerful figure, may the world listen to him!

If they had a life perhaps they wouldn't choose to become terrorists.

The Kurds, I discovered, were America's allies when it was a full-on battle in the east, but then Mr Trump did a back flip and wiped these poor people by withdrawing his troops out of Syria. They are now set upon by the Turkish army, who have shown them no mercy. The Kurds are people who are spread throughout many countries; they are a diverse race of people, now to be treated as the enemy is disgraceful! The saying 'all is fair in love and war', who wrote this? America, you have failed these people! This was the basis of my book called *Pimchan and Amira*. Amira was a young Kurdish girl whose life is typical of the life they are suffering at this very moment in Turkey and Syria. This is a heartbreaking read, but it is what is happening in our world today.

I have found out all I needed to know, so now my computer can have a well-earned rest. I tried to turn it off, but wait ... something is flashing on my screen: 'In lockdown'. What did this mean? I try to move my cursor but nothing is happening, what am I meant to do? Why was this happening, what had I done? This message was still flashing on my screen. In desperation I rang a friend for advice, who just happened to be a policeman, maybe he could help? He asked me what had I been using my computer for and when I explained what information I was extracting, he had the answer. "You have unlocked a secret code, alerting intelligence of your movements.

These are the websites terrorist suspects visit." Did this mean I was a 'suspect terrorist'? Intelligence had locked me out of my computer, so they could come in and search to see why I was spending so much time on the subjects of terrorists, as well as nuclear weapons.

I felt sick. Did they really think I was involved in terrorism, when all I was, was a writer? The 'lockdown' was to last for twenty-four hours in which my computer could not be used. My God, how did I become embroiled in all this mess? Was my nosiness leading me into all sorts of trouble? All I was doing was satisfying my own curiosity, this is called current affairs surely! Then I had a terrible thought: would I make headlines? I could see it all unfolding: 'Retiree taken in for interrogation for breaching the security code'. From this day forth, I vowed I would stay away from weapons, bombs and terrorists!

But on this subject, these codes are put in place and are crucial in helping police foil terrorist plots before they actually happen. Like silly me, as soon as the code was unlocked, intelligence goes into the suspect's computer and places a watch to see what is unfolding. Someone did mention that next time I left the country, I would appear on the screen at the airport as a 'watch' suspect. This frightened the living daylights out of me. To think in a few months, we were going on our annual holiday to Australia.

Australia, here we come!

Our holiday had arrived and so had the fear! Would I even make it out of the country? Would my name flash up on the airport security system when I put my passport across? Would I be led into an interrogation room for questioning? So many things were going on in my head, my eyes were darting everywhere, I was uneasy; would this make me a prime suspect? I felt dodgy, did I look dodgy? I had to take control of myself, I hated flying, but all this other stuff had taken my mind to other place. So far, so good!

As we were proceeding through security, my soul mate set the alarm off, so he was asked to step aside. He was then asked to take off his shoes and his belt. "The reason the beeper went off is because I have two artificial knees. I shouldn't have to take off my shoes?" he told the woman in his authoritative manner. The reply came back, "I'm sorry, sir, but you have to follow the procedures that are in place. Please do as I ask." I looked around and everyone was asked to do the same, which they did without a fuss. I couldn't believe my soul mate drawing unwanted attention my way, I didn't need this! Were we ever going to get out of New Zealand? This made me feel like a 'targeted terrorist' trying to cross the border. I was furious with him, why couldn't he be like everyone else and do as he was told? Not my man from Mars! One could have thought he was concealing something in his shoes by refusing to take them off. I knew he wasn't, but the authorities didn't. The word divorce flashed through my mind several times.

Finally, we were on our way across the ditch, without either of us being detained. Sometimes I wished my soul mate was just plain ordinary, but then, would he have been the one for me? The answer being ... who would know? Would my life have been so different? Perhaps I might have ended up in a council housing estate on the bones of my backside. One can only surmise!

Of course, to settle my nerves after this horrific experience, I needed to have some retail therapy while in Aussie. The Coolangatta markets were on the next day, being Sunday. It attracted plenty of people, all eager for a bargain, but this was not a bargain market; everything was a little more expensive than the word 'market' implied. Of course it was; here were tourists to target, they had plenty of dosh, they had come to spend. This was the stallholder's chance to extract a little extra money from their victims' purses and wallets, this was their livelihood, they had to survive!

It was a delight to see people's talent being showcased, such a variety of skills and treasures. My eye was drawn to the wearable stalls, one in particular had taken my eye. Of course, it was a designer label, one-offs, but the clothes were beautiful. I searched through the racks, everything was to die for ... not really, they would be no good to me dead, wrong saying. I will reword that phrase: they were begging to be taken from the racks and proudly displayed on a happy victim. Was I one of these? Of course I was!

Being size sixteen, I didn't have the same selection as a size twelve to choose from. This was discrimination. Why punish us voluptuous women? We have the same feelings as a size twelve person. It is just that we appear different but we are not! We all have the same body parts, the only difference is our skin has stretched, not our fault, of course; this is caused by that aging thingamajig.

The clothes reflected the designer's image, which was a mixture of hippie and heaven. The mixing of colours and textures was outstanding, in fact beautiful. I took three tops off the rack in my size and disappeared behind the curtain, where there was standing room only, but this didn't deter me, I was on a mission, I was there to buy. What a decision, I couldn't decide which one looked nicer than the other; this only left one decision: take all three, then I wouldn't be disappointed!

Having made this decision, I was about to leave when a lovely slim lady popped into the stall with her pal, a little white poodle. She had come to pay off some of her hire purchase, which was kept in a bag with her name on, out the back. As she walked past the racks a new long coat had taken her eye, so she lifted it down and instantly fell in love with it. I knew that feeling only too well! Next thing I had a leash in my hand and was in charge of a strange dog. She tried it on and asked my opinion, so I gave her the thumbs up, it was so her. Off it came and joined the rest of her clothes backstage. Was she ever going to pay everything off, or would she just keep buying?

Then a thought flashed through my mind: oh my God, if I lived here, was this a version of me? (A much slimmer one, of course.) Would I have a stash of clothes out the back, waiting to be paid for, before I could collect them? This brought on goose-bumps; was this the truth, staring me in the eye? Thank goodness we only holidayed here once a year, otherwise I might have ended up a victim, just like her!

It had come time to say goodbye to Australia for another year. Now all I had to worry about was the thought of not being allowed back into my own country. We put a couple of bananas in my soul mate's backpack to eat at the airport, before the flight. Four hours later we were in Dunedin airport checking through customs, when a dear wee beagle came up to my soul mate and sat down beside him. His handler was there in a matter of minutes. "Excuse me, sir, do you have any food in your bag?" he enquired. My soul mate was very indignant about being questioned. "No, I don't have any food in my backpack, I would have put it in the bin if I did." "Well, I must ask you to open your bag, as my dog has indicated that you are carrying food." With this he sighed and reluctantly opened his bag. Guess what? There were the two bananas we were meant to eat at the airport, before our flight. Instead we settled for a breakfast muffin, which looked more inviting ... until now? When was guilt ever going to disappear from our lives? It took a long time for me to shake off the feeling of being a 'suspect'.

Peace of mind

Today, I am relaxing in my favourite chair. Beside me is my little Buddha boy and surrounding him are my speaking stones, by speaking, I mean each one carries a message: compassion, wisdom, gratitude, strength, etc. When I pick them up, I feel a connection, they take me to my happy place, where my mind is free from everyday woes. I purchased these after I learnt to meditate, as the messages are powerful reminders of what meditation is all about.

I meditate religiously every morning for half an hour, mainly before I eat ... empty stomach, empty mind. This is the beginning of every day, a routine I have carried out for the past nineteen years, and never faltered on. For me this is a commitment, it gives me the feeling of being able to discipline my mind, which puts me in a calm place. From this commitment my mind is able to cope with whatever comes my way. There is a certain calmness that comes with meditation; it is all about quietening the mind and as the mind stills, a great many things are accomplished. It brings balance, rest, repair and can take us to deeper levels. I have experienced this!

One day while meditating I was sitting in a sunny position where I could feel the rays of the sun sending warmth throughout my body, making me feel totally relaxed. I felt serene and at peace, then something strange happened, something that I had never experienced before. I could not feel my limbs, it was if my arms and legs were no longer part of me, but it was the next phase that took me to another level. My head left my body and hovered above; I was having an out-of-body experience. Thank goodness I had read about this, so knew not to panic, just to let it happen, as I had reached a deeper level of meditation. This left me stunned for the next few days. I couldn't talk to anyone about this, who would believe me?

After a few days I did, however, decide to share this with my soul mate. But I should have known how he would react: he thought I had gone completely mad, in fact stark raving mad, perhaps it was time to commit me, to a place where others went who imagined weird happenings? After this I kept it pretty much to myself, although I did share it with my best friend, as she was into meditation, although not as committed as myself. She longed for this to happen to her, but it never has! I came to the conclusion that my dedication to meditation allowed me to have this amazing experience. It did happen, only that once, but I will never forget it. I feel I can share this with you, my readers, as you can think I am mad, even bonkers, whatever, and I won't hear what your thoughts are. It was an experience I will take to my grave, perhaps that is why I think differently to most other people. Now I understand how the Tibetan monks can sit for hours, even days in a trance and be transported to higher places.

This all came about nearly twenty years ago, when I talked my soul mate into attending a lecture by Dr Ian Gawler at Otago University. What a job, he refused so many times, I begged him to do it just for me, as I thought it would help him and me to understand what lay ahead for us both. Ian had opened the Gawler Clinic in Melbourne to help cancer patients and their partners prepare for what came next. He was a cancer patient himself and had miraculously self-cured; he couldn't offer a cure to others, but he could help in other ways with diet, exercise and meditation. The mind needed to be calm so one could face each day as it came.

To commence his lecture, he asked us all to join him in a short meditation. We were at a loss as to what this entailed, as were many others attending. Someone was brave enough to ask how to meditate, so Ian took us through, step by step, explaining how to block out all thoughts that were in our minds, to be switched off from the outside world. Once told how to do this, it came easy to me, as I loved the silence and emptiness of my own mind, and being able to close off to outside pressures. It was a release, a dedication, that over time has taught me how to manage stress and pain.

May I add, my soul mate didn't get anything whatsoever from meditation, so he never pursued it, but of course he was different, he was the spaceman from Mars. Had they not heard of perseverance up there? What did they learn? Twenty years later he is still with us, probably because he said he was never going to share his wife, his toothbrush or his fortune with anyone, therefore had to hang around, just to make sure this didn't happen.

My life changed dramatically from my meeting with Ian Gawler. After the lecture we both spoke and I felt an immediate connection; just his presence and what I had taken on board from his lecture left me feeling fulfilled. I learnt about the power of positive thinking, to love myself and not let anyone make me feel less than what I am! I went off and bought inspirational books, which I read until my head was filled with joy and compassion. I loved the authors who wrote these books and thank them inwardly for taking me to a place I didn't know existed. One of my favourite authors was Wayne Dyer, who had gone through hard times, but found himself and shared his journey with his readers. He became a much sought after inspirational author. He believed in himself, this was where the power of positive thinking paid off for him. From each book I read, I took out little passages that resonated in my heart and entered them in a diary of my own, which has become a treasure that I can call upon when I feel it is needed.

Here are a couple of my favourite sayings: 'If you don't go within, you go without', 'You cannot purchase happiness and inspiration, these are what one brings to life'. I know that the heart is wiser than the head, trust it and follow it! We are never too old, never say never, it is only a word, nothing else. It means 'at no time'.

Back to my little Buddha boy, he is sitting with his legs tucked under his butt and reading his scriptures. My big Buddha father is outside facing the rising sun, sitting on a stone-filled pedestal, which I made especially for him, so he can meditate in peace all day long. Each time I pass, I rub his protruding belly, letting him know he is not forgotten! He is not the prettiest of Buddhas, but he is the old wise man, one who has been around for a very long time, one who brings a smile to my face and a calmness to my soul.

My son, who has spent time in Thailand among the monks and temples, told me the monks are ordinary young men who at an early age became novices to embrace their culture and the scriptures. Some leave and live a normal life, but others are prepared to go without, to serve and earn a higher place in the afterlife. They will remain poor in wealth, but rich in faith. Each morning they do their 'alms walk' around the villages, each carrying their offering bowls in which people, as poor as they may be, always contribute food. The food is then taken back to the temple to where everyone is fed. Any leftovers are available for the poor to come and collect. Humble is how one would describe these people.

Another one of my everyday rituals is called 'tapping'. This is an ancient Eastern relaxation technique and teaches one to tap special places on one's body. It is big in America and is being introduced in schools there, where young children participate in the classroom before they start their lessons. I am a relatively new student and am only one year into this, but am committed. It only takes five to ten minutes to tap the nine pressure points and it has a calming effect. I combine this with my meditation; these two rituals are my self-time, which I reward myself with each day. I am a happy, positive person; this is made possible by my commitments.

What are my beliefs?

I didn't quite know where I stood in the religious realm until my soul mate and I decided to get married. His family were Roman Catholic, mine were divided; my father was a Methodist and my mother was an atheist. This is where the religious divide began. Either way, if one family got their way, the other family would not attend. I could not understand why religion came before their children's happiness, surely children came before religion? Isn't this what religion is all about ... family? To save any embarrassment we eloped. I was of age, so didn't need my parents' consent. This turned my thoughts on religion from a positive to a negative.

My next encounter with religion was when our eldest son was six years of age. His friend at school was a Catholic and attended special lessons and my son wanted to go with him. I thought long and hard about this. My soul mate had been baptised a Catholic and I was of no religion; was it time for me to take his faith, for the sake of the children? This I did, which meant our registry office marriage was not valid, so I married my soul mate for the second time, in a Catholic church. It was a very quiet affair and only my father knew. He was fine with it, but advised me to hide it from my mother, she must never know, so this became a secret. I had to hide the truth, so again religion played a sad part in my life.

Several years later we adopted our little daughter who was only thirteen days old, this being our next encounter with the church. Her birth mother left one request, to have her baptised a Roman Catholic, and this request we honoured. For many years religion was never part of our lives, but did it need to be? We knew what rules to live by, they were the same for everyone, whether religious or non-religious! Everyone was created equal; religion does not define who we are. That is up to ourselves.

As the years passed by, I became more interested in spiritualism. To me spirituality is broader than any single religion, as it looks inward, not outward! I read books written by the Dalai Lama and came to understand what the monk's contribution to life meant. They didn't ask for money, no one got rich, all they needed to survive was to be fed. Each day they meditated, which to them is the art of observing without thought and this became a big part of their lives. They also became teachers to the boys of the poor areas who couldn't afford to pay to attend school.

They gathered at the temples to be taught the basics of life as well as the scriptures.

A saying by Buddha: "When you travel, go with those who are better than you or at least equal. If there is none, go alone, do not travel in the company of fools."

I have learnt about wisdom; to have good sense and judgement, to choose to spend time in places that inspire me and associate with people who uplift me and who I feel comfortable with. Self-worth is more meaningful than net worth. Stories themselves are medicine, they have such power, we only need to listen! Here is a passage from a book I read, which inspired me, written by Clarissa Estés: "A healthy woman is much like a wolf, she carries everything a woman needs to be and know. She carries stories and dreams and words and songs; she is both vehicle and destination. She is a painter, writer, dancer, thinker, peacemaker, seeker and finder, as in all art, she resides in the gut, not in the head. She is ideas, feelings, urges and memory, she is the source, the light, the dark and the daybreak."

These words are so beautiful and portray the female species as something special ... which we are! This describes the very essence of a woman. We hold families together through good times and bad. A mother's bond goes deep within and is rarely broken. Of course, we are all of these, we are from Venus ... a planet second nearest to the sun, also a Roman goddess of love, this is definitely us! Our menfolk are from Mars ... fourth planet from the sun, and a Roman god of war, yes, truly male. No wonder we are warm, loving creatures, we draw more warmth from the sun as we are closest. Men just get what's left; not really, we love our menfolk (most of the time). Thus the explanation men are from Mars and women are from Venus!

Gosh, off the beaten track I have strayed, but this is what is called living. Nothing ever goes to plan, we deviate, we lose our sense of direction, but we are allowed to, it is our privilege to live this way. It is called freedom, freedom to roam, to dream, to do anything really, this is our time in life!

Special places to visit

We all have somewhere special we would like to visit in our lives. I had two places that I longed to see, in fact, they were 'sacred' must-visit destinations, but I only managed to get to one of them. This was brought to light as I watched television last night, there it was. So far it has been my favourite place on earth, this being 'Uluru'. What treasured memories it brought back to me. I loved the vibes I picked up from this precious rock. I touched it, even kissed it and whispered my special prayers against its earthen red walls. My soul mate and I walked halfway around it with a guide, who explained what caves were used for certain occasions, but we did not walk upon it. To me it was there to be admired, not to be walked upon. I thought this was wrong, as Uluru was scarred by a walkway with posts and ropes put there for the safety of climbers. It detracted from the very essence and meaning of this heritage site. The wind came up strong in the afternoon, so the rock climb was closed, much to the bitter disappointment of many people, but safety was paramount. Arguments started between the would-be climbers and the rock's caretakers; this was not what this scared place was about, it was a place of peace, not a place to conquer!

A decision has been made to close Uluru to climbers for ever, this I applaud! And to learn the rock had been polluted by people urinating while climbing this majestic landmark really upset me. What did this do to the drinking holes used by the Aboriginal tribes that still visited for special occasions? How short-sighted and devastating; why were people so stupid, surely, they knew this would lead to unwanted consequences?

I remember when we arrived seeing Uluru painted red by the sun, it was spectacular to say the least. It had totally lived up to my many years of dreaming, now it was alive before me, it was beautiful! The tour we were on was spending the whole day at the rock, and staying for the sunset. This meant we would witness it changing from red to gold, then turn grey as the sun went down. On sunset, the bottles of bubbly were cracked open and we all charged our glasses to witness this wonderful changing of the guards ... sorry, changing of the colours. It was like a miracle unfolding before us and once the deed was done, Uluru turned grey and cold. How could something so beautiful and warm turn to a rock without a soul?

But all the tomorrows would see it rise again and again in its majestic glory and its secrets would be shared with all those who took in its beauty without destroying its very essence. To close the walk to the public was in my mind the right call, as Uluru must be preserved for future generations to visit and learn of its history and share all its secrets.

I have several treasures as reminders of our memorable visit to my 'sacred rock'. I love the earthen colours, the desert reds and oranges, the blue of the sky and all the dots that tell the stories, not that we understand; only the local Aboriginal people know these meanings, but these are their secrets and stories to savour.

My other sacred place is in Peru, high up in the mountains. It is the remains of an ancient village, which was built by the Incas in the 15th century. It is called Machu Picchu. Inti, the sun god, was the chief deity of the Inca people. Machu Picchu was abandoned in the 16th century for unknown reasons, perhaps a plague or a war? The terraced ruins are shrouded most of the time by a mist drifting down from the mountains, adding to its mystique, as it reaches up to the heavens. I will never physically visit this place, but I can feel its presence, and see it in my mind, I have even dreamed of having been there. Sometimes dreams can take us places, they can become a reality in our minds. This can be made possible by the power of positive thinking!

By the shake of a hand

The most prominent piece of art in our cottage hangs in pride of place on our wall away from the sun's rays. It is a screen print of Rembrandt's *The Night Watch*. This brings back memories of a true gentleman, one of the nicest men we were lucky to have met in our lifetime. This is a true story of two grown men, who on the shake of a hand sealed an everlasting friendship. It all began when my soul mate was building a holiday home in our local town of Clyde, when he was approached by a gentleman who wanted an identical house built on a section he owned. He asked for a rough estimate of the cost, which my man gave him on the spot, as he knew what the one he was building was costing. The two men sealed the deal on the shake of hands.

Six months later, when the keys of the house were handed to the new owner, he wanted to know the final account. Nothing had been written on paper, so any price could have been asked for on completion. But my soul mate, being a man of his word, told him the original price still stood. He could not believe what he was told, never before had he handled a business deal this way, especially on the shake of a hand. As it turned out he owned an upmarket furniture showroom in South Dunedin called Butsons Furnishings. He was Mr Buttar, Ernie as he wanted to be called, but out of respected, neither of us would use his first name, so he was always addressed as Mr Buttar. He told us to come to his store and choose anything we liked, in appreciation of our honesty and ongoing friendship. On our next visit to Dunedin we called at his showroom and were blown away by the upmarket pieces on display. As we walked around, my soul mate's eyes were taken by a very large painting hanging high on the back wall of his store. Mr Buttar explained that it was a screen print and had been in his store for eighteen years. Many admirers had asked to buy it, but it was not for sale. There were only eight in the world, and two had come to New Zealand, but one was damaged so it was recalled. It left us intrigued after hearing its history.

Two hours later we left the shop empty-handed as we didn't know as to what price we could spend. We were humble people and would rather him give us something. Several days later we received another call from Mr Buttar asking us to bring a trailer next time we came to Dunedin as he wanted something taken back to his Clyde house. A fortnight later we left the trailer at his store, as we had business to do in town, but by the time we got back to his store it was near closing time. The trailer was sitting at the back of the store all loaded up, so we let Mr Buttar know we were picking it up, as we wanted to get home before it got too dark.

When we arrived home, we parked the trailer in the packing shed so the package would be safe. The next morning the phone rang: "Hello, Kelvin, Ernie here, that package you took home last night, where is it?" My soul mate told him it was safe in the shed and was still on the trailer. "I want you to take it into your lounge and unpack it, this is my present to you in appreciation for all you have done for us," then he hung up. We looked at each other; no, it couldn't be, could it? We rush out to the trailer and struggled in with the package, both eager to unwrap it. Once unwrapped, there before our eyes was Rembrandt's *The Night Watch*. The very screen print that many people wanted adorning their wall, now it would adorn ours. This holds precious memories for us both, as Mr Buttar is no longer with us, but his memory lives on in our cottage. He was one of life's true gentlemen.

Race day

Today I am in the spare bedroom making it presentable for our guest who is coming to stay. There is still one box to unpack; it has been sitting there for a couple of months and now the time has come to unpack its contents. Out comes the framed photos of Petty Lane, our long-gone galloper. In the family home they had their very own wall of fame, but not so here, we have run out of wall space, so they will be put behind the rocking chair in the meantime, out of sight, but not out of mind. She brought with her joy, heartache, celebrations and tears. I remember the day she qualified for the 'Valachi Downs', a big race at cup week at Riccarton. I will take you through that race, I remember it as if it were yesterday: 'The adrenalin is pumping at a hundred litres a second and my voice is loud, it is almost a scream, was this me I could hear? Surely not, no, it must be that silly lady next door. I looked her way, no, she was silent, this was not her horse leading the field, it was our Petty, yes, that screaming voice belonged to me! What a fool I must have looked, as I crammed as close to the rails as I could get without them collapsing, but I didn't care, Petty Lane was in the lead, I had to cheer her on. Just a few more metres to go and she would take out the big race, as well as a big prize purse, in front of thousands of people attending Cup week. Would you believe it, on the outside lane appeared someone else's donkey? Surely not, no, it couldn't ... but it did. Petty was pipped at the post.'

My image of fame was short-lived, it was over in one second! Where did that stray donkey come from? I waited hoping there would be an inquiry into the race and the first horse would be relegated to second place. I waited, but the siren never went. Never mind. I had to console myself, second place was definitely better than last, imagine watching your horse limping home over the finish line in last place.

This is the joy of racing ... one never knows until the race is over! Horse racing was in my blood; my dad was a big gambler, our only outings entailed going to the race track with him, this was our family picnic day. But that is another story! We followed all Petty's races, she brought us an immense amount of joy. She had twelve wins in her racing career, so yes, I yelled myself hoarse many times and drank to her success. Those were the good old days! When I watch the racing today and see the owners and trainers so emotional, the yells and screams along with the oh no's, this is all part and parcel of the racing scene. It is such an adrenalin rush, but outsiders must think the racing fraternity is mad and should be locked up and put away ... or put down? Not so!

No wonder I enjoyed 'Cup Day at the Races' held in our Residents Hall. Sweepstakes kept selling out, and new ones were created, so I bought tickets in most of them. One of the gentlemen from the village had the cheek to asked me if I had a gambling problem when he saw all my tickets. I replied, "It certainly looks like it" and we laugh it off. But the end result, I doubled my money, we had two winning tickets and a second. Great day! Oh, how I miss the racing fraternity!

Back to grass roots

Today it is wet, in fact it is very wet. The thunder and hail they forecast has arrived, it is a mini storm, but there is blue sky in the distance, so hopefully it will pass as quickly as it arrived. Shortly we will be on our way to attend a ukulele choir held at the village centre. All the ladies are from our village, so one feels it would be nice to support them. This is one of the privileges of village life; the entertainment is there for those who want to attend, with no cost. There is no driving involved, as it is all on our doorstep, what could be better than that? One of the nicest things about all this, the patients from the care home are brought out to participate with the cottage owners. I brought this up with my soul mate and told him when my turn comes to go into care, I couldn't think of a better place to be. The staff are bubbly and friendly and the outlook onto the bowling green and surrounding gardens are picture perfect.

The ukulele choir has begun and everyone is joining in with the singing. The old songs are the favourites as everyone knows the words. This is the key to entertaining the elderly, they feel they are part of this modern world. It brings them out of their comfort zone, perhaps a little sense of adventure, or a nostalgic trip back to the past. But whatever, today they are enjoying themselves.

I spoke with a lady sitting next to me, as she was from my home town and had moved into the village with her husband, but he had since passed away. She stayed on in her cottage, but due to ill health is now in the care home. She has her own room and is very happy. It is lovely to hear what the residents think and to know they are happy; it says a lot about the village and its management. Our village is privately owned by a local family; it is not a corporate affair. The residents I have spoken to are all happy. I have not heard an unkind word spoken by anyone and this makes for a happy environment.

A controversial treasure

I just cannot let this story pass; it has to be told! My most unusual treasure has caused controversy in our home from the day it arrived! I secretly congratulate myself every time I look at it, as it is one of the only battles I refused to back down on. I stuck to my guns against all family members and so far I still have it, but for how long remains to be seen. My son-in-law — no, he's not that, he's only my daughter's partner and until he marries her he cannot inherit this title — says he has a buyer for it. Of course, encouraged all the way by my soul mate, but two hundred dollars? I'm not selling it for a measly couple of hundred bucks. Not that I paid that amount for it. This is how it all began.

Our neighbours were taking their flat-deck truck to an auction and called in to ask if we would like to come. My soul mate was not into auctions, but me, I was into anything, especially if there was a bargain to be had. Off we went, just the three of us with an empty truck. Did this spell disaster before we even started? On our arrival we went our separate ways to explore what was on offer. I wasn't there five minutes when I spotted something that I fell in love with. No, it wasn't a man, but something more exciting, a huge wooden sculpture of a ball within a ball. It stood waist high and was unique. This caused me to stop dead in my tracks; this was mine, it had to be, I loved it! I would probably have traded in my soul mate to have this!

But the burning question: how much was it going to cost me? I thought long and hard about this, it looked very expensive, would I have enough money in my EFTPOS to pay for it? What would my soul mate think? If he had telepathic powers, the words 'leave well alone' would be coming through loud and clear. But he wasn't blessed with these powers, thank goodness, so how was I to know what he thought, not that it mattered one iota. Then I remembered I had our trusty old credit card in my purse if I needed it, so price was not going to be an issue.

I never ventured far from this item, I just had to stay close in case someone stole it from under my nose. My neighbours came along and asked if I wanted to have some lunch, but I refused, I had more important things on my mind; lunch wasn't even in the equation. The auction was in full swing and things were being sold left, right and centre, but it was still a long way off my (to be) prized possession. It was now 5 pm and the crowds were thinning out; this was playing right into my hand. Suddenly the auctioneer appeared beside me and asked for a starting bid for my ball. Someone yelled "Fifty dollars". This was the start. I didn't bother showing my interest, that would only push the price up, so I decided to wait to start bidding around the five-hundred-dollar mark. Eight hundred would be my final bid.

At one hundred and seventy dollars the bidding suddenly stopped and the final hammer was about to fall; I yelled and raised my hand. "Final bid of one hundred and seventy-five dollars to the lady in front with the curls." Then I heard the thump of the hammer. Was it mine for so little? I was in total shock, I knew the price of these wooden sculptures, this had to be the buy of the century. The owner, who I knew, came over to me and told me I had a steal at that price. He had it carved by a Queenstown artist ten years prior and it had cost him four hundred dollars. The only reason he was selling it was because he had sold his orchard and was moving to a smaller home and had no room for it.

He explained that it was a bough from a huge tree and had been sculptured into a ball, then a chainsaw was used to carve out the inside leaving a smaller ball that was separate, but could not come out. This was where the problem began. It came with its own carry cradle, which took four people to lift, because it was solid timber, therefore weighed a ton. Thank goodness there were enough men around to help lift it onto the deck of the truck. My neighbours had bought very little. Just as we were about to leave the auctioneer asked me if I would take the final lot, consisting of two wicker chairs, table and other bits and pieces, for the princely sum of five dollars. Why not? There was plenty of room on the truck. As we were driving home my neighbours told me this was worth a cup of coffee at ours, to which I agreed.

As we backed up our driveway, my soul mate appeared. "Someone's had a good spend-up," he quipped, thinking of course it belonged to the neighbours. "Yes, your wife did well, most of it is hers" was the reply that came back. "Don't even think of loading that junk off here," said my soul mate in one of his less formidable voices. With this, his services were called upon to help lift the ball off, then came the rest of the items amid a string of curses. Suddenly our neighbours were in their truck speeding down the driveway. What happen to the promised cup of coffee? They could see the air was so thick, it nearly had to be sliced with a knife. This was no place for them, they were out of there!

I suffered fiery glares from my soul mate for the next week: fancy bringing all that junk home, and that wooden thing, where was it going to be displayed? May I tell you it took pride of place in our lounge and received many accolades from visitors, due to its uniqueness. Until we shifted, our neighbours and I still had a snigger behind my soul mate's back over the auction and the promised coffee that didn't come to fruition.

Now, of course, it is us that has downgraded to a smaller home, so my soul mate thinks it's time for my controversial treasure to be passed on to someone else. But I am standing my ground. Although it is positioned behind my lounge chair and barely able to be seen, I will not let it go without a fight, and for two hundred bucks, you would have to be joking. This wouldn't even cover the suffering I have endured over the years, trying to keep my wooden ball!

You are never too old to live the dream

Don't ever think you can't live the dream; anything is possible if you set your mind to it, age is no barrier. I have always wanted to dabble in the share market, in fact I have dreamt about it for a long while, so here I am at seventy-three living the dream. "Will I be rich? Will I be poor?" Does it really matter? The experience is all I want to be part of.

My soul mate has been in the share market for some time, as he bought shares when the power companies offered them to the average New Zealand mums and dads. The bank interest rates were so low, forcing people to look elsewhere to invest their money. I wanted to buy and sell shares, take a risk, be a bit of a rebel! My brother set me up on the computer with a share company. What a lot of poppycock we had to go through. A copy of my passport had to be signed by a designated official. Thank goodness I was able to call on someone in the village. I needed my IRD number, and I had to supply a recent bank statement with my name on it. Was it all worth it? I asked myself.

Now the questions started: what shares was I going to buy? But I didn't even know myself. The next week I spent perusing the paper each morning just to see what was on offer. My soul mate kindly advanced me some money and along with my book revenue that was sitting in the bank doing diddly-squat, I was ready to break into the financial scene! I was green, I knew nothing about shares, just that I couldn't afford to buy blue chip ones as they were too expensive. I had to start at the bottom, at the 55-cent mark, and hope they would multiply many times! Was I on my way to becoming a millionaire? If this was so, would my life change? I asked myself. The answer came back as no, I was happy with myself the way I was, I was at peace, no amount of money could change that, because peace came from within, it could not be bought! As long as I was able to sit in the sun and feel its warmth penetrating through to my bones, this was as close to heaven as one could get.

My new job each day was to check my computer to see if my share portfolio was increasing or decreasing. So far, I am three hundred dollars up. I'm not climbing the rich list very rapidly. The other day my son arrived from Alexandra and asked how my share portfolio was going. "Just a minute and I will pull it up on the computer." "No need for that, Margaret, I will put an app on your phone, then you can pull it up any time, anywhere." "Can you do that?" I asked in bewilderment. Within ten minutes, there it was on my cellphone. Thank goodness I have managed to participate and keep up with modern technology, I have to admit it does make life a lot easier!

Modern gadgets, what next?

Yesterday my brother arrived to stay for a couple of nights. During a conversation I told him of my sleeping woes, that once I got up for a toilet stop about 2 am, I couldn't get back to sleep, so lay awake for the rest of the night. "Surely you can go back to sleep, perhaps you are imagining it?" he told me. "Yes, she is, I look at her and she is asleep," added my soul mate. "Okay, we will settle this once and for all," my brother intervened, as he could see an argument in the air. "I want you to wear my special watch to bed tonight and I will tell you in the morning how much sleep you had. Not only that, I will be able to tell you whether you had deep sleep or light sleep." I almost fell off my chair laughing; don't be so silly, I told him. But true to his word, that night I had to wear his magic watch to bed. Again, I had a disturbed sleep and felt I hadn't slept a wink.

In the morning when he came out, he had his cellphone in his hand. "Okay, Margaret, give me the watch so I can get the reading. How much sleep did you think you had last night?" "Not much as I was awake most of the night." Here was the moment of truth, I would prove I was right to my soul mate, then he would have to be gracious in defeat! "You had three hours of deep sleep and two and a half hours of light sleep. You woke twice at these times." I looked at his phone in disbelief; they were the exact times I was awake because I looked at the bedroom clock. Then why did I think I wasn't sleeping? Was it all in my head?

Perhaps I was too engrossed in my writing and couldn't switch off. I was the one who had to acknowledge defeat, which hurt! "Right, I am going to get you one of these, so you can see that you are in fact getting some sleep. It will also give your blood pressure, heart rate plus a lot of other details." I didn't argue, I was beaten at my own game!

So now I am the proud (confused) owner of this modern piece of equipment, which, I ashamedly admit, sits on my side table in the lounge, day after day, not in use. The fact being I don't do watches; they tell the time, which means pressure, and I don't do pressure any more. My working life was built around pressure; that era is done and dusted. Time is not important to me. I have learnt my mind or my soul mate will let me know when things need to be done. I live in a timeless zone where there are no time limits and no pressure. Nothing is impossible when you live the dream.

My life today is very simple. How I have changed, even shocking myself and my soul mate. Clothes used to be my first love; my man came a close second. It wasn't until we shifted and my walk-in-wardrobe was no longer available to me that I realised just how many pieces of fabric I owned. Where on earth did I think I was going to wear them? One can only wear one item at a time. Now I am on a 'no-buy scheme' thus limiting myself to the odd new pen, which I have noticed is by far a lot cheaper than a pair of jeans. But to be fair, pens are a lot smaller! I even wrote a verse about my wardrobe, which I have put at the back of this book.

All I need today to be happy is my pen and pad as this is my escape to many different experiences. One minute I can be the heroine, the next a villain, I can fall in love as often as I choose, which brings me back to that all-important word: memories! These we all share in common; by common, I mean we all have our own memories, not common memories as such, as mine are probably a lot different to others'! But whatever our memories and treasures, be sure to hold on to them, as they are our journey back to our past. We can choose which ones to hold on to and which ones to let go … we have choices!

Family

Now to the 'second last' treasure, an important one at that, a family photo taken in 1983 when our eldest son was eighteen, our next son fifteen and our daughter nine years of age. What young-looking parents we were then. What happened? We don't look at all like that today. Age can be a cruel reminder of one's past! Our daughter, who is now about forty-four, visited us the other day and stood in front of the family photo and remarked on the outfit she was wearing. "How did you get me to wear that horrible dress?" "I probably had to bribe you" was my answer, which was quite on the cards, as she hated being dressed up. In spite of her comment, I told her she looked very feminine, of which she shook her head and turned away; the word feminine didn't seem to register.

I was thrilled to think we had a little daughter that I could make pretty dresses for, but instead I got a tomboy who shunned the idea of looking pretty. Even today this still applies. I can remember her father and I escaping to Australia for a week's holiday on our own, and I asked her what clothes she would like brought back. This was her answer: "I don't like colours, dots or stripes." So, I bought her white T-shirts with a little pattern on the pocket to take away the plainness. On our return and upon giving them to her, this is what I was greeted with: "Mum, you know I don't like squiggles." It was then I learnt that there were going to be clashes between us, we weren't going to see eye to eye on everything, in fact our thoughts differed on many things!

But because she was adopted, of course we were going to be different, our genes were not the same! Deep down I always had the feeling that we had to dig that little bit deeper to make her happy in case she didn't like us as parents. Also, the underlying fact that her birth mother might want her back one day, so from the day she could understand, she was told she was 'special', in fact the 'chosen one'. We grew as a family and she had a good life with us. Although at times things were a little difficult for her, especially in her teenage years when we moved to Australia, as she had four different schools in six years. Adjustment played a big part in her life in more ways than one.

The fact of our life being that if we had not adopted our daughter, we wouldn't have had any grandchildren. She gave us two lovely grandsons. As my man says with despair, "The boys are useless, they are only here to have a good time, but what of the family name, it is going to disappear?" If nothing else, their lives were indeed colourful. The eldest stole his best friend's wife, who was from the Philippines; the next son married a Japanese interpreter and after eight years of marriage they separated, so he went to Phuket for a holiday and met a Thai girl who he eventually married. So, we have four foreign grown-up step-grandchildren, twin Filipino boys and two Thai children, and now we are known as 'the league of nations'!

With life comes surprises by the bucketful, as we never know from one day to the next how many things will end up in the bucket. Life, they say, you can never plan, or change; things happen in that one moment in time and one must accept and grab every moment that is available. No complaints from me, our life has been like a rainbow: very colourful with no ending in sight.

My new life in a retirement village

There are so many benefits that come with living in a village with people similar to yourself. Everyone understands what grief accompanies us as we grow old together. The differences in age, from sixty to ninety, bring mixed experiences; some people of ninety can be just as bright as a sixty-year-old, they haven't let that spark get lost in their latter years. New residents bring with them new personalities and this makes for a more diverse community. Village life is not a holding pen waiting for God, which I originally believed; we are in a safe and controlled environment where we can live without fear of having drug houses or undesirables as neighbours. Contrary to a lot of people's opinions, residents of a retirement village are not beyond living life to its fullest, enjoying all that is on offer to them, be it entertainment, bus trips and, most important, friendship.

I did not appreciate how caring and gentle elderly people could be, as I had never really associated with many. One of our neighbours is ninety-four and lives on his own. He is one of life's true gentlemen, always asking after us, who happen to be nearly twenty years younger than him. We are amazed at his choice of shirts, they are so modern; he has not lost the ability to keep himself respectable and modern. He intrigues me!

On our other side live a couple in their late eighties who are just as caring. At the slightest sign of rain in comes my washing if we are away. I have never experienced this kindness ever, and to think I had to wait until we came to live in a retirement village. Our street is full of delightful people and the conversations we have bring laughter aplenty! I enjoy and cherish every moment I share with these residents, and feel we have been accepted into their family.

As I look back at our life before becoming a resident, I now realise how sad it would have been for us as we grew older, as the younger generation are busy living their own lives. We as elderly citizens are not part of their thinking, we sadly become the 'forgotten', that is until the word 'money' surfaces, then we are suddenly remembered! Isn't it funny how certain words can trigger off a sudden memory revival? To be part of a caring community and have everything right on your doorstep is a certainty for a happy retirement.

For me, coming to terms with growing older was not

easy, but I am at peace with myself, so self-acceptance now plays an important role in my life. I have learnt with each day to seize every glimpse of happiness that comes my way and make the most of these moments, as once they pass, they cannot be retrieved.

One must never let go of their independence, even as a married couple. Independence is important, as it keeps us in touch with a sense of ourselves as a separate entity and when the time comes, when one of us is left without our partner, then we don't have to say "Who am I, now that I'm not so-and-so's wife?"

I am a reader, a writer and most importantly a dreamer, a housewife and now a nurse. My husband's favourite saying "I married a wife, now I've got a mother" is qualified by my answer, "I married a husband, now I have a patient". These are not hostile words but spoken with humour and feelings, which we both laugh together over, because the truth is something we can't hide from! Reality has to be faced honestly. Something must have held us together for fifty-five years ... but of course, it was and still is my happy nature and my way-out imagination! I read this saying yesterday and thought how appropriate: 'Before you can be a good two, you need to be a great one, find self-love first.' So, so true!

The end

On finishing my story, the end has arrived. This can have two meanings: the end of my story and the end of life. Neither can go on for ever as we have to move on. I would like to share with you how I overcame my fear of death. Many years ago, I had a near-death experience and this is what happened.

My family had all been called to be with me as I floated in and out of consciousness. I was at peace, a calmness had descended, then before me a mist appeared and, in the mist, stood a figure in a white shroud. His hand was outstretched waiting to take mine, but in the distance, I could hear people calling my name and I opened my eyes. It was not my time to leave. I learnt through this experience that we are never alone; someone is there for us and this is when my fear of death ended. Do not be afraid to let go when your time arrives to leave this life as another awaits. It is a peaceful transition, there is no pain; the only pain lies with those left behind. We were never ever going to be a permanent fixture on earth, time is only lent to us for an undisclosed period, so we must enjoy and embrace each day.

This near-death experience triggered off a rigorous research programme as I wanted to know if other people who had had this experience came to the same conclusion as myself. To my surprise, we all had similar experiences and we all laid to rest the fear of death.

This story has been written on my memories and by revisiting my past. Please take time to look around your home, at your treasures, then you too might be inspired to put together a story on your life. Remember, 'Tomorrow is promised to no one.'

Here my story was ending, but ...

Instead a whole new scenario is facing us, one that no one could have foreseen. It has arrived as an unwanted visitor, the 'coronavirus'. The date is Wednesday, 25 March 2020 and at 11.59 tonight a Covid 19 Level 4 lockdown is being put in place. Our world has changed for ever!

Who would have thought in this day and age with all the technology available to us, that this virus couldn't have been stopped before the whole world became its victim? We are so advanced in many areas but this has defied all odds! Now the whole world and all within are in the grasp of this pandemic.

How life can change in the matter of a few days, from being in a happy, secure place to one of feeling at a loss and very vulnerable. The illness itself is, of course, a huge worry, but the side effects on businesses, incomes and job losses could lead to an economic meltdown.

As retirees over seventy, we will not be affected money-wise, unless one plays the share market, but we are all at a vulnerable age in which the virus can cause severe health problems; we are in the high-risk bracket. Life will not change too much for the village residents, apart from that personal contact with each other; this will be missed, as will the cancellation of all activities. Instead of a handshake or a hug, we are now relegated to a meeting distance of two metres apart. At this distance we can still share a joke and have a laugh, life has not ended, just distances extended. We are now in Level 4, which means we must live in our bubble for the next four weeks and follow all new instructions as they develop.

A changing life, day by day

Yesterday, the day before the Covid 19 lockdown, I ventured to the supermarket to replenish my fresh fruit and vegetable supply. I along with many other shoppers had to join a queue outside the supermarket, all standing two metres apart (by our assumptions) waiting for people to leave before we were allowed to enter. There he was, in his mask and gloves holding a loud-hailer announcing when new shoppers were allowed to go through the door. I likened it to an outer-space experience; all we needed were the flying saucers, then it would have felt real!

After being allowed to enter the supermarket I couldn't believe what greeted me. My thoughts (which at times are pretty imaginative) took me back to when I had heard my mother talking about the depression days during the war. There on the shelves were signs 'Limit 2 per person', that was if the shelves were not already empty! What was I experiencing, is this what the shelves looked like in a depression? How sad it must have been for families back then, as the families were larger, thus more mouths to feed. There was certainly no government assistance then, not like today. How on earth did they survive?

Has this happened to let us experience how hard and sad past periods of time were, which made suffering a part of everyday life, but brought people together and taught them to care for each other? Were we becoming a selfish society wrapped up in our own little worlds, wanting the biggest and best of everything, not stopping to even think or care for neighbours and people who were less well off than ourselves? Is this nature's wrath spelling out to us all, be warned, this is only the start? Now everyone is in the same boat, rich and poor alike, so together we have to obey the same warnings sent to us all. This life will not discriminate between the wealthy and the average Joe Blogs, this is a levelling-out process, money will not buy any favours, we will all suffer together. In fact, the poor will adjust much quicker than the wealthy as they don't need the finer things in life like morning lattes, dining out and social drinks; their lives are less complicated.

Today an eerie silence has descended the village and surrounding streets; no vehicle noises have penetrated this stillness. This is day one of Level 4 of the coronavirus lockdown and many of the village residents are out and about enjoying the sunshine, filling in time as all village activities have been suspended. The ones sitting in the sun on their outside seats are engaged in conversation with passers-by, as everyone is eager to discuss the present situation. Many questions are asked, but very few are answered, because no one knows what lies ahead. We have ventured into uncharted territory!

Being a writer, my mind went to making up a billboard to lift everyone's spirits. I found my old painter's easel in the garden shed so I dusted it down ready to put it in our driveway. But to my dismay my soul mate disagreed with me, so in the laundry it remains. This is what I wanted to say: 'Just because we are in lockdown, let us discard the word "down" — depressed, unhappy, lower place — and replace it with "up", indicating moving upwards where happiness and positivity reign.' This was not to be so!

I have just been informed by a committee member that a nurse from our local medical centre is visiting this afternoon to give us all our flu injections, in the protection of our own homes. I thought this was an excellent call, proving that us elderly are well cared for in these times of uncertainty. Also, the village management have arranged for residents to leave their carry bags with their names on and a grocery list at the Residents Club and they will arrange for our shopping to be picked up and delivered back to our cottages. How wonderful is that? None of us will starve. It is like living in a five-star hotel, only we don't have young porters for room service (wishful thinking) but we do have young shoppers and delivery persons.

Our cottage is situated at the end of a street, actually on a T junction. Just along from us is the rubbish bin enclosure so we see most of our side of the village who bring their rubbish to be emptied, so of course many conversations pass between us. Today was especially social because everyone spent the day either in the garden or tidying their sheds, all looking for a way to occupy their time and take their minds away from the ongoing Covid 19 broadcasts.

Several residents wanted to know if I was writing them a letter, of which I replied, "If you could call eighty pages a letter, then yes." But one inquisitive person wanted to know if I was writing another novel and did the village people get a mention? I told him 'yes', then of course he wanted to know if I mentioned names, of which I told him 'no'. 'Why?' he asked. "I don't want any libel cases against me, so names are a no-go." "But we will know if it is us you are writing about," he answered back. "Yes, you will know, but try and prove it," I told him. By this time, he could see that I was right up there with the protocol on my rights pertaining to writing. If he reads this, he will know who he is, no one else will, so it will be his word against mine.

Some residents are at a loss as to how to fill in their day as they are usually at golf or bowls. But all cars must remain parked up for the next four weeks. This is only day one; what will day two, three … and the rest bring?

My share portfolio — and the rest!

Earlier in my story I mentioned I had decided to play the share market, to buy and sell shares, and to maybe become a wealthy woman! This is an update. Sadly, my dreams have been badly quashed, as my shares have plummeted downwards, not spiralled upwards as I expected. I am momentarily disappointed; the economic downturn due to the coronavirus has impacted hugely on the share market leaving many of our shares worth less than what we started with. Even the fancy app on my cellphone put there by my son, to tell me of my nett worth, has been untouched for two weeks. The shame of it all! But at this stage to sell would be a travesty; one will live in hope that once this is all over the market will correct itself ... then perhaps my patience will be rewarded handsomely! Here we go, dreaming big again!

My soul mate's shares have also taken a tumble, which

does not please him, as his hobby is to make money, not lose it. But them's the breaks. There are winners and losers in all facets of life, and at the moment we are the losers! But hey, we can still laugh. I will change this, I can still laugh, although a half-hearted one at that!

Today is another day, in fact day two and like yesterday nothing much has changed, and probably will not for the next three and a half weeks. I have been for my daily walk, meeting likewise residents who are out and about, airing their frustrations. I'm sure the footpaths will be worn out by the end of four weeks, with the pounding they will get, but all for a good cause. We all share the same thoughts on village life, how lucky we are to be here in this environment where we are all safe and cared for. The worries of the outside world can pass us by and we will remain happily tucked up in our own little bubbles. A neighbour from further down our street walked up to put his gardening rubbish in the bin. He called out, "Good morning," of which I corrected him by saying, "I think it is afternoon." "Is it?" he questioned, then looked at his watch. "Good Lord, so it is, it's two-thirty." Time means nothing while in lockdown! This made me inquisitive so I went and fetched my best friend, my dictionary, to look up the meaning of time and here is what it revealed: 'past, present and future as a continuous whole'. What a long explanation for a simple word, no wonder we forget time, as its meaning is far too long to remember. Especially for us older folk as we have a wealth of knowledge stored in our brain and we can't be expected to remember everything, in fact a lifetime of information is hanging in there! Some things just have to remain outside our sphere (field of activity).

Last night on TV Three we watched a programme on the coronavirus and it was very interesting. It explained in depth just how unknown to mankind, even to the virus experts, how devastating this strain of virus is. Because it is a new strain no one knows how to contain it, or how long it will be around. It is known to start from droplets so self-isolation is a start. Whether we can ever get on top of this, there are no answers; the uncertainty leaves everyone, including the top medical teams, very worried.

Since writing the above I have new information on Covid 19 so I will add it here. A coronavirus is a type of virus that can cause illness in animals and people. Viruses break into cells inside their host and use them to reproduce themselves and disrupt the body's normal functions. This virus from Wuhan is one that has never been seen before this outbreak. Coronavirus is a 'sister' of the SARS illness that hit China in 2002. Coronaviruses are a family of viruses that infect a wide range of different species, including humans, cattle, pigs, chickens, dogs, cats and wild animals. It is known to be able to occasionally jump from one species to another. According to scientists the virus almost certainly came from bats. The first cases of Covid 19 came from people working in or visiting a live animal market in Wuhan. Although the market is officially a seafood market, other dead and living animals were being sold there, including wolf cubs, salamanders, snakes, peacocks, porcupines and camel meat. The genetic make-up of virus samples found in patients in China is 96% identical to a coronavirus they found in bats. However, there were not many bats at the market, so scientists say it was likely there was another animal which acted as a 'middle man', contracting it from a bat before transmitting it on to a human. As yet that animal is not confirmed. A reason for concern is nobody has any immunity to the virus because they have never encountered it before!

One must ask oneself, is this what has happened in the past to earlier civilisations, were they wiped out by viruses? Up until now, global warming took centre stage, but that has been upstaged by our present dilemma. Where to from here? We must stay positive if we are to get through this; united we stand, divided we fall!

Today is Sunday, 29 March, a sad day as we have lost our first New Zealander to coronavirus. This has been a much talked about subject; as each resident passed each other on their daily walk, we all expressed our sadness, as this has brought home to us all just how vulnerable we are! Because this death happened on the West Coast, a remote part of New Zealand, it was a surprise, as it is sparsely populated and quite isolated. Nowhere is safe from this dreadful virus, it finds its way to every corner of the world.

MEMORIES AND MOVING ON

On a lighter side I met a new couple who had shifted into the village on Thursday. They were meant to come in on Friday but because of the Covid 19 lockdown they managed to get the carriers to shift them late Thursday night. Not like our friends who had arranged to shift in this week; they had to put everything on hold because of the 'stay-at-home policy'. They will not be shifting in until the lockdown has ceased or reverts back to Level 2 and no one knows how far away that is. Many lives have been put on hold.

Oh, another wishy-washy day, cloudy with the odd break of sun, ruined by a chilly wind, so my soul mate decided the best place to be was snuggled up in bed, so that is where he lies! I would love to have stayed, but I live a very disciplined life. First comes my exercises to try to bring movement back into my hip muscle, followed by a half hour of meditation, then ten minutes of tapping; these routines set me up for the day.

This afternoon I was speaking to my neighbour, who came out from Holland as a young lady, and I mentioned about being in isolation for the four weeks. She told me about her life in Holland during the war and how they had endured five years of curfews. "Five years, how did you cope?" I was shocked! "It was our life; we were just kids and we had to accept it." This made four weeks of lockdown seem as insignificant as a pimple on a pumpkin, and a huge one at that! What was I worried about? I find her a very interesting person.

As the days go by

Today is Tuesday, the last day of March. Our daughter came and picked up our car and her partner took theirs to the supermarket, as only one designated person from each bubble is allowed out to grocery shop. She wanted to do our shopping so I left our grocery list and the keys to the car on the seat, so off to the supermarket she went. It is amazing what transpires from a lockdown; it makes the younger generation think about their elderly parents, as this act of kindness would probably not have happened otherwise. I know they lead a busy life and we were lucky to have been thought of today! Now we are stocked up on fresh fruit and vegetables along with milk and bread.

But the one item most needed and wanted was not available and that was pepper. We both like salt and pepper with our meals, so it will be sorely missed. Oh well, if that's all I have to grizzle about, then I'm lucky. I don't know the origin of pepper, so I will make that my mission this afternoon. I'm sure Mr Google will be able to help me; he knows a lot of stuff!

Well, Mr Google was very obliging, so I found all the information I needed. I will share this with you as it is quite fascinating. *Piper nigrum* (black pepper) starts its life as berries in a clump on a flowering vine. Originally a native to South India, today it is grown throughout the tropics. There is a myth that groves of trees in India and the Caucasus Mountains were guarded by poisonous serpents. In order for the pepper to be harvested, the trees had to be burned, driving the snakes away and in the process turning the original white fruit black.

Pepper was originally traded on the Silk Road, the most well-known trade route used many years ago. But it was such a desirable spice that Italian traders could essentially set their own prices. This led to a pepper status, as a luxury item in medieval Europe. On his home journey Christopher Columbus stocked his ship's holds with what he believed to be peppers and brought the spice all the way back from the West Indies, only to discover his ships weren't full of priceless peppercorns but worthless chilli peppers. At one time pepper accounted for a whopping 70% of the international spice trade. Today, Vietnam has emerged as the world leader in pepper production.

Perhaps this explains why there is a shortage, as at the moment only urgent supplies are being sent from these countries. But isn't pepper urgent? I hope with all this new information I will be able to answer more questions on *Millionaire Hot Seat* or *The Chase*. My soul mate is amazed at some of the answers I come up with, but then my head is constantly in a dictionary. Yet simple everyday things simply don't appear when I need them. I am a worry unto myself!

It is 1 April, April Fool's Day, but warnings have been sent out to not play pranks regarding Covid 19. It is a beautiful sunny day and everyone seems happy; it is amazing how the sun can heal the heart. I try to sit outside each day as I love the sun's warmth making its way through to my bones. It is a feeling of complete fulfilment. This is day seven of lockdown; day by day time seems to go slowly, but when I look back and see that a week has already passed, one wonders where it went. Hopefully the next three weeks go by just as quickly. Each morning brings a new day and each day something different happens, not any one day is the same. Like people really, we are all separate individuals who bring diversity to others' lives. Imagine if we were all the same, how boring life would be. We wouldn't have to leave the house, as all we would see was a mirror image of ourselves. How did I get to this silly conversation? I must end it now.

Today I received a message from my friend in

Australia and this is how it went: 'Did you know China started the coronavirus purposely, so when all the Aussie businesses go broke, they will come in and buy up Australia, eventually owning it all.' A frightening thought to have China as a neighbour. I would rather have the Aussies even though they hide sandpaper in their jocks at a cricket match.

Another lovely sunny day and a lot of the residents are out walking and catching up with their daily natter. On my walk today, I rushed home to get my camera, as I came across an interesting settlement of mushrooms or toadstools, I'm not sure of the difference, but they were putting on a lovely display. I took several photos from all angles and have them stored on my camera. A verse will be forthcoming in the near future! They were at various stages of their short life, some just making their entrance, others were fading and falling apart with old age ... a terrible thought. But as in all aspects of life, it comes to us all whether we are a mushroom or a human, nothing or no one is exempt! Our time on this earth is a gift, so let us embrace it and enjoy every moment!

Friday again, oh how I miss our 'happy hour' as it was a joyous time with plenty of laughs! Never mind, when it happens again, boy, will we all celebrate! Something positive to look forward to. Today started cloudy and cool but as the sun came out it warmed up to 16 °C. It was a quieter day, not so many walkers. On my walk I did encounter two gentlemen in conversation, one was sitting on a seat in his vegetable garden, the other one was ready to hand out some cheek. "Be careful of this one, she writes stories about us village people." "Yes, you are already in my book but without a name," I replied. I didn't stop to hear what was said, as I have learnt that listeners never hear good about themselves.

Censored — 18 years and over

Today is 4 April and it certainly doesn't seem like a Saturday. No families visiting, the cars are all parked up, no building going on, the village is silent, in fact we feel deserted. The sun came out but there was a sharp nip in the wind. I only did half a walk today and met up with a well-known character in the village. We chatted then had a great laugh on a subject that happened to come up in our discussion. It was centred around a TV programme called *Naked Attraction*. "Oh my goodness, did you see all those naked men? I didn't know there were so many different penises," she said. I thought for a moment then answered, "Obviously you didn't have a good look around when you were young," I was teasing her. She looked at me in total shock, not expecting that answer from me. Quickly I assured her that I hadn't either, I was just as shocked as she was. So, we established that we were both innocent when we were young. Today is so different, it would not be the case with the young ones as they have been around. But us oldies, we are still learning, but it was cause for a good laugh. Our conversation didn't end there, but what came next was private between ourselves, but it brought a lot of hilarity. One would have thought we were giggly teenagers, but we would not have been discussing the same subject back then.

A conversation came up at one of our happy hours a couple of weeks earlier when I told about Kelvin surfing the net, then calling to me to come and have a look at what he had found. There before me on the TV were six coloured capsules with six nude males; of course my reaction was to burst out laughing. "How on earth are they allowed to put that on TV, it is X-rated, surely?" I stuttered. But on saying this, I stayed and watched the programme to the end. No one else at our table had seen the programme, well, that's what they said, but who would own up to watching such a show in front of others, especially people you didn't know well? They would think you were a pervert!

Not long after this discussion I noticed the programme *Naked Attraction* was no longer available on Channel Three. It could only be seen as a paid programme, but rightly so, as it was a little bit (no, a big bit) out there!

This was how the person I stopped to talk to found out about *Naked Attraction*. She said it was Kelvin and I who introduced her to it, so now we are the village villains?

MEMORIES AND MOVING ON

This took me back many years ago, when the men used to tell jokes about little men. Inquisitive me asked my soul mate why they always told these jokes. This was his explanation: "When the maker made man, he hung their private parts on a line. Then he told them to pick which one they wanted, but first he thought it only fair that the little men be allowed to choose first. So, they ran to the line and the only ones they could reach were the long ones, so they grabbed them; this only left the small ones for the tall men." My question had been answered and forgotten about, until today.

Later in the day while I was sitting on my outside writing seat, my friend from along the street stopped and we picked up where our conversation ended earlier in the week. She was only about nine years old when Holland was caught up in the war. Some of the older girls, dating age, had affairs with German soldiers. There were good and bad soldiers, as with any men, but these girls ended up suffering at the hands of their own communities. They were marched up the street to where crowds were gathered, their hair was shaved off and their scalps were painted red. Sadly the ones that had the misfortune of becoming pregnant often committed suicide because of the shame they brought to their families. It must have been sad to have been young during the war years, as a man is a man whether he is German or Dutch and love is love, whether right or wrong!

I received a phone call from a lady in the village to say

she had read my verse booklet that she had picked up from the Residents Club and thoroughly enjoyed it. This was the second call I had, so people seemed to be enjoying them. It is nice to get feedback, then I know I can continue to put new ones together for the residents to enjoy.

Sunday, the day of rest. 'Really, what is different about today?' I asked myself. Nothing, as one day runs into the next while in lockdown. Oh yes, daylight saving ended; instead of having breakfast at ten o'clock, we had it at eleven o'clock, but ten o'clock old time. There is a reason for late breakfasts at our home: my soul mate has to take four chemo pills at least an hour before he can eat. I wait and we have breakfast together; this allows me to finish my meditation, empty stomach, empty mind.

As I was watering my garden and lawns a couple walked past and we spoke. "Are you bored?" she asked. I told her I wasn't as I always had plenty of writing to do. She proceeded to tell me they watched Billy Connolly last night. I was so surprised as I thought his language would have been too coarse for them. "My husband was watching it in the lounge and I was in the dining room, some of the words I heard were a bit over the top," I replied. She told me she didn't understand a lot of the words, but at the moment any kind of comedy was welcome, as we all needed a laugh. How true! You can never judge or presume things about people you don't know!

MEMORIES AND MOVING ON

It has been a busy day, so many things to write about. A group of people have gathered on the street, some had just come back from a walk, another was putting rubbish in the bin, and I was sitting with my tell-all book. The conversation started on hot cross buns, then of course stories followed, and we all had a laugh. A good friend was going to make her own buns, but was worried as the yeast was out of date, so she has promised to report back to us as to how they turned out. Then lunch came into the conversation, so we all had to report what we each were having. By this time several people had left. My friend was having avocado on toast, our neighbours had pickled pork sandwiches made and we were having scones. I had baked date and sultana scones this morning at my husband's request. It took me back to the first batch I had baked in my village oven. My soul mate made a promise to a certain person that in payment for a good deed he had done, he would be rewarded with some of my scones. I just wished the ones I made today were the scones he tasted, as my first batch was a disaster; not a real disaster as such, but they definitely weren't my best. One day when the lockdown is over I will prove that I can actually bake a satisfactory scone!

Last night, I decided to ring my girlfriend in Australia to see how she was coping as she had recently lost her husband. With the lockdown she would be on her own, so I thought she would be finding it lonely. Of course she was and it had hit her hard, as she was an artist and a very social person. "You know, Marg, I miss my friends not being able to call, or being able to go out for lunches. I didn't realise how lonely I would be," she stated. "But what about Bill, it must be sad without him?" I asked. "Oh yes, I now have to do the grocery shopping and cook my own meals, I even have to put fuel in the car, gosh yes, I really miss him." I could hardly contain my laughter, but that was Kath, she hadn't changed one little bit! She and Bill lived completely separate lives; he was a headmaster, the domesticated one, she was the social butterfly. Sadly, Bill had been diagnosed with cancer and had only lived for six weeks after that. "You know, Marg, I gave Bill a wonderful send-off, everything was of the best, he would have been so proud of me. Nothing was spared, I gave him everything he would have wanted." This made her feel good, so helped heal her loss. "But I must tell you something funny. Bill was cremated, this was his wish, and when it was time to pick up his ashes, you'll never guess what happened." I shuddered to think what was coming next. "On the way home, we stopped off at a hotel to celebrate Bill's life. We took him in with us, then we ended up having a meal followed by a few more drinks then we went home. The next morning someone asked where Bill was, no one knew until we realised no one had picked him up off the table and brought him home, he was still at the hotel. I flew into a panic, what if he had been put in the rubbish bin? After all my good work, I had let him down. But to my relief he was where I left him. I'm not going to let him escape again, he is now where I can see him." I burst out laughing; the blame lay with poor old Bill! We had been friends since primary school, then boarded together at the YWCA in Christchurch in our heyday. She is someone whom you would love as a friend, her thinking was way outside the square, but she oozed fun, nothing fazed her, not even Bill's death. Things just 'passed over' and blew away, tomorrow was another day! Our friendship has lasted all these years and although we are totally different, we are both involved in the arty-farty scene. I would be the more 'homy' one of the two of us, she is the social out-there one!

There they go, the three likely ladies who meet and walk each day together. First, they hold a meeting to see who chooses where to go, that is if they remember whose turn it is. Most days they meet outside our cottage so I am usually privy to their conversations. I just let them know I'm the chairperson taking the minutes of their meetings. There is a lot of pre-planning that goes into their daily walks, as they try to find new paths to travel down. Two have walking sticks and one has a walker, but this does not deter them. They are taking the lockdown in their stride and dealing with it handsomely. The younger generation could learn a lot from their tenacity ... go to it, ladies! Among them is a mother hen and she lives 'up the hill'; as she tells everyone proudly, she is the organiser, the cheerleader.

Gosh, Monday has arrived again; it has greeted us with

a cloudy outlook, but is still mild. There go the likely three on their daily journey. I missed their meeting this morning as I have just come back from my walk, so don't know their plans for today! My neighbour across the street is down on her knees trimming her edges, she hardly gives them time to grow before she is attacking them again. I envy her being able to kneel. It is impossible for me at the moment to do so, but I am hanging on to hope!

It is funny to hear what people miss most while in lockdown. A gentleman who lives down a block, and is always away in his car, must be finding it hard not to get behind the wheel; the temptation must be great. We engaged in conversation and he said he was missing his oyster meal at the Best café and a decent coffee; however, we did agree on an item of necessity that was available, and we both had some in stock ... wine! Oh yes, I agree with him, the Best café oyster and fish meal is definitely the best in town! The side plate of bread and butter, how good is that, and sitting at Formica tables on Formica chairs takes me back to my childhood days when this furniture was the fashion, everyone owned them! This proves one important thing: décor does not matter one iota if the food is good!

And on it goes!

We are now up to Tuesday, 7 April and it is overcast with spits of drizzle. Not many walkers today, really it is an inside day so that's where everyone seems to be hiding. My publisher has sent my new book through to Amazon so now all I have to do is wait for the proof to be couriered to me. I chose for it to come by fast CourierPost, which takes only five days compared to three to four weeks by ordinary post from Australia. Mind you, it is expensive, for one book $63, but I can't wait for it to arrive, that is the excitement of any new publication, just to see it in the flesh, your own creation. Once I read it through and give my approval then my publisher puts it on Amazon as an e-book and a print book. Then the damage is made known to me, by way of ... his account!

Although there is not much happening around the village, there is worldwide sad news. The British Prime

Minister Boris Johnson has been admitted to intensive care with Covid 19. Two English nurses have died at the age of thirty with Covid 19 while attending patients with the virus and they each have left behind three children. How tragic when medical staff leave their loved ones to care for the sick, and end up leaving us! They are indeed the brave; we will pray for their families. While people in Europe and the US are dying in their hundreds each day, we in New Zealand, so far, have been spared such losses.

My soul mate's oncologist rang him today to check that he was coping okay. He told him to stay indoors and not mix with people because of his zero-immune system, only to sit outside to get a bit of sun each day. This is what he said: "Kelvin, if you get this virus, we cannot save you," which were cold hard facts to hear. "I have kept you alive for eighteen years and I don't want to lose you now." These words were a little more comforting! But it just brought home the seriousness of Covid 19.

Another day has greeted us, the sun is shining and the village is alive with residents who are taking advantage of this lovely weather. After being stuck indoors yesterday it is time to air the cobwebs and enjoy nature. They are all making their way to the Residents Club with their shopping bags with their names on and their grocery lists inside. Our management have arranged to do our shopping for us, then deliver it to our cottages. How wonderful is that? I couldn't believe how many bags were on the floor; how on earth were they going to shop for so many people and not get people's orders mixed up?

In our mailboxes today all the residents received a newsletter, again explaining how important it was to obey the rules and stay two metres apart. This had been overlooked by some residents, so it has been brought to our attention.

Today is Thursday and our groceries were delivered before lunch. How on earth did they fill all those bags in one morning, when people had to line up in queues outside supermarkets? One can only express our thanks to the wonderful village staff and management. No payments were made as this would mean contact outside our bubbles, so we will be sent out an account at the end of the month. How good is that?

The Easter that wasn't Easter!

Good Friday and no one could attend any church services. How strange! It was a silent eerie day, although the weather was kind, so some Easter joy was bestowed upon us all. Sadly, we lost our second citizen to Covid 19. The walkers were out and about early today, I suppose because there was nothing much else to do, but enjoy nature.

My neighbour came past and we again picked up on our conversation on wartime Holland. She stood at the end of our driveway and we corresponded from our usual distance. I was seated and couldn't ask her to share my seat or we would be breaking the rules, but we are used to this by now. It is the way of life at the moment. A bit like wartime itself? She was telling me how the young girls of dating age were rounded up by the Germans and taken to paddocks for the day. Sisters were separated into different paddocks. This was to attract the young men who had gone into hiding to avoid being recruited by the Germans to become soldiers. If the young men wanted to make contact with their girlfriends they would go to the paddocks, where the Germans lay in wait. The temptation of the young girls was too much for their Dutch boyfriends; this was a cunning ploy by the Germans. The girls were not harmed and were allowed home later in the day. I enjoy what I am learning about wartime in Holland, it is very interesting.

Everyone was out in their gardens today as there was very little else going on in the village. This is the Easter that doesn't seem like Easter, no visitors, no cars leaving their garages and no planes flying into Dunedin Airport, but we are saved by one mode of transport and that is the trains. They rattle past behind our village; thank goodness something is normal. Sadly, we lost another two citizens to Covid 19 today, taking the total to four.

As I was on my walk this Sunday morning there was mention of two Easter bunnies seen in their 'onesies' in the village. Sadly, they didn't leave any Easter eggs at our place, so we have had an eggless Easter, first time ever. Covid 19, you have a lot to answer to! The likely three are meeting to arrange their walking route today. Accompanied by a walker and two walking sticks, these ladies are a laugh a minute. Another resident with her walker and a couple walked by, so it became a meeting of the clan.

They wanted to know if I was taking the minutes of the meeting — of course I was!

This week was hampered by cold weather so not a lot of action. Being Wednesday, all the residents did their grocery bag and list drop-off at the Residents Club. When I took my bags down there must have been at least fifty bags waiting to be filled. Again, I wondered how on earth were they going to sort out all this shopping. But true to form, our deliveries were dropped at our cottages at 10.30 the next morning. Well done, staff and management! We love you all! Friday was another wet, miserable day and more sad news: the death toll in New Zealand is now eleven Covid 19 deaths.

Today is Saturday and the morning being wet and cold, how was I going to fill in my day? I needed a project to keep my mind occupied, so here it is. On reflecting back over the last three weeks of lockdown, an interesting pattern has formed. A positive finding from the lockdown period has been brought to my attention by interacting with village residents and the outside community. I asked our residents what they would think if the Government extended the four-week lockdown by another two weeks and they said it would not worry them. But when I asked my friends (our age) outside the village, there was a completely different outcome: they would be upset with an extension, as they were feeling trapped and cut off from the world.

This made me think. The village residents were more

agreeable to whatever the Government's decision was. Is this because we have each other and know we are in a safe environment, therefore can leave our cottages and walk around the grounds knowing we would meet others we could talk to, so loneliness was not a problem? Of course, we all miss the family interaction, the supermarket shopping and activities, but no one anywhere has these privileges during Level 4 lockdown. All residents share the same thoughts: we are so lucky to be living in a village environment, where we are cared for. Management look after our grocery needs as mentioned earlier; when the flu vaccination first came out, nurses from our Mosgiel health centre came to the village and gave us our vaccine outside our cottage doors, how wonderful is that? Especially when we watched the 6 pm news on TV 1 and saw the line of cars with elderly people waiting to get to the health centre at Mosgiel for their vaccines; some were lucky, others missed out. My conclusion, in a crisis like we are facing, we as village residents feel grateful for our choice of lifestyle; we are part of a wider family who all look out for each other.

The sun came out this afternoon so the village was alive with walkers. A lady from just up the street stopped and sat on her walker for a little rest as she had been for a walk, so we got talking. We discussed the lockdown, then she told me that she spent her fifth birthday in hospital as she had contracted polio. For the next nine months she was hospitalised. Then she went on to become a nurse. In the 1950s there was another outbreak of polio and she worked as a night nurse looking after three patients, one in an iron lung.

She also remembered the tuberculosis outbreak as she had visited the sanatorium at Waipiata with a family member. My father spent seven years as a patient in Waipiata from the age of twenty-one to twenty-eight, before he married my mother. Dad had photos of the men sleeping out on the veranda with the windows wide open in frosty weather, so they could inhale the cold air into their lungs. It just takes little bits of conversation to bring back memories from the past.

While we were talking, another lady from up the street joined in our conversation, which switched to our grocery deliveries yesterday. This brought a wave of hilarity from the three of us. One of the ladies in her eighties had put on her list 'panty liners' and what arrived was a packet of sanitary pads. So, what we were actually laughing about was that a male staff member delivered her shopping, and if he was the shopper, he would be forgiven for getting it wrong! But we had a laugh at whoever's expense! She wondered if she should contact the management and get them changed, but our manager is a male. We told her just to keep them or give them to someone else. I could visualise our manager's face; it would change from a blushing pink to a bright red if he was confronted by this. The innocence of the elderly! I then mentioned about my order: I asked for a leek and received a bunch of spring onions, but that's okay, they are both linked to the onion family. Obviously, our shoppers are not seasoned diehard shoppers, but we forgive them, they are doing a great job. We know who you are, you are wonderful souls, thank you! Never a dull moment in our village!

Each day for the last week one of the male residents has walked sprightly past our cottage. I have lost count as to how many times a day he does this, and now it has got the better of me, so I will have to find out why. Is he training for a marathon? Today is the day to pry, so I waited eagerly on my tell-all seat until he appeared. "Excuse me ... why are you doing this and how many times a day do you go past here? Are you training for a marathon?" I asked. "I walk the perimeter of the village five times a day and it takes me just over one hour. I'm doing this to keep fit." There was my question answered. But he is a slightly built man, no excess weight; why did he punish himself so, for what reason? I asked myself.

Gosh, it is that time again to take our bags to the Residents Club with our grocery orders. Several people had gathered and we all got chatting, all agreeing how lucky we were to have such a service. Then the funnies started. One of the ladies put on her grocery list last week that she wanted cheerios (meaning small saveloys) and instead received a packet of cereal called Cheerios. But we are not complaining, we are having a lockdown laugh, as we are really truly grateful!

On the way home we meet up with the likely three and their aids. It was one's birthday and because we were in lockdown she couldn't celebrate. Not that she minded as her birthdate is surrounded by two very important birthdays, the Queen's and Shakespeare's, so she was chuffed to be in the company of such notable people.

Today is Saturday, 25 April, Anzac Day, an important day for us all to remember, but with no public gatherings everyone has to remember the fallen in their own way. I have an extra person to think about today: it would have been my mother's birthday so it has a special meaning. Sadly, I couldn't visit her graveside with my usual bunch of flowers as we are in lockdown and many miles away, but I can still hold her memories close to my heart.

I have been waiting on a parcel to arrive from China and decided it was time to track where it might be. Two months have passed and I have heard nothing, so today is the day. One day while on Facebook I found a site advertising clothes, beautiful tops and dresses, for very reasonable prices. I couldn't believe how cheap they were. Each day there they were begging to be bought, so I caved in and made a purchase. I ordered three tops and paid by debit card. Within a few minutes I received confirmation with a tracking number so I could trace my order.

A few days later, it was time to make a move and do some tracking, so on to the computer I went and put in the tracking number, to which it told me it was on its way. Then to the side of this website I saw that many other people were wondering what had happened to their parcels as they had heard nothing. 'Oh, my God, not another scam surely,' I muttered to myself. I then decided to look up the huge list of scammers and guess what? There was a similar company, number 1000 and something, on the list. I knew then I had to say goodbye to my purchases, but as the saying goes, 'If it sounds too good to be true, then it probably is'. This was my first purchase online to China and will be my last! Thank goodness it wasn't going to break me, instead just dent my pride, once again! If I keep going at this rate, soon I will have no pride left.

Today we have five cases of Covid 19 and a total of eighteen deaths, but hopefully we are still on track to Tuesday's Level 3 status. Not that it will change our way of life one iota; we get no liberties being over seventy. But life is comfortable for us, so we are not complaining. Although right now people are craving escapism, wanting something to feel good about! We have all been thrown a curve-ball, but it is one we are learning to handle. This pandemic will make us see life through different eyes.

Sunday has come around again and the village is very quiet. As the sun comes out more people are starting to move around, which is great to see that they are using all that nature provides. I am leaving for my daily walk. On my way I meet my elderly neighbour and we walk together with our handy aids, his walker and my crutch. Where would we be without our needy supports?

A little further on, we meet my neighbours from our other side who also were making the most of a lovely afternoon. It is strange as we don't often see each other (they are a lovely couple), so to meet on the other side of the village seemed quite strange, but nevertheless we engaged in conversation. Then we each headed off in separate directions on the rest of our walk, until we came to the stream where my companion made a suggestion for us to sit and have a natter. This we did, talking about all sorts of things, as he is in his nineties and is a very interesting gentleman. While we were sitting there the marathon man (as I have named him) passed us on the first of his five rounds of the village. When we decided to carry on, we only made it a couple of hundred metres further on, when we were passed again by the marathon man on his second round.

As we neared the new cottages being constructed, we stopped and wondered what the going price would be, along with other questions. We were then joined by another lady so it was another sit-down affair; they sat on their walkers, which left me to stand, but I was happy. And then guess what? The marathon man was coming towards us on his third lap. I called out to him, "We won't see you again, we will be home before your next lap." My famous last words. "We will see," came back his reply. Would you believe we were only a few metres from our properties, and bugger me, here he was again. It was just too much so a lot of banter was had by all. One thing for sure, on his next and final lap we would definitely be home unless a catastrophe happened in the next ten metres. Thank goodness we were spared the embarrassment.

Out of the blue today I received a phone call from a friend that I hadn't heard from for at least three years. It was lovely to hear from her; she rang to say they had shifted into a Summerset retirement village in Christchurch two years ago. She was happy to hear we had done the same and we both agreed it was the sensible thing to do at our age. This was her second marriage as her husband had passed away when she was in her early seventies, and she had met Ted at dancing classes. She moved out of her flat into his beautiful home, where they lived until they moved to the retirement village. Ted will be one hundred in a couple of months and is suffering from memory loss, but she is looking after him. They have been together for fourteen years, so I was upset to hear that when he dies, she has to leave the village. I presume he bought their cottage and must be paying the associated costs while they live there. Does he or his family not think that she deserves to stay on until her life ends, as acknowledgement for looking after him for all these years? She will have to go and live in her flat with her son and his partner, and will miss the social life she has at the village along with all her friends. How sad.

Our Covid 19 Level 4 lockdown has seen nineteen deaths to date.

Tuesday, 28 April 2020 ... Level 3

We have now reached Level 3 lockdown and a beautiful day has greeted us. The sun is shining down on us today to help us celebrate this milestone, not that anything much has changed from Level 4 for us over seventies. But at least we get to hear the traffic starting to move about, as limited tradespeople start back at work. It feels a bit more like some sort of normality has finally returned to our lives. On my walk this afternoon, as I passed the new block of cottages under construction, it was great to see the guys back at work, as the buildings have been at a standstill since Level 4 lockdown. The men seemed happy, as plenty of banter was passing between them.

Silence is okay for a short period of time, but then it becomes daunting. We all long for normality, even a new kind of normality, in fact any sort of normality to return, then we will feel as if we are part of civilisation once again.

When all we know is suddenly taken away and we find we have to adapt to a new way of life, it takes time to adjust, but we have no other choice than to accept what we are faced with. We have all survived and a new appreciation of life has greeted us ... what will be the new norm? No one knows, it will unfold day by day! Covid 19 has changed our world for ever, there is no way of foreseeing what lies ahead; these will be challenging times. Being the resilient creatures that we are, we will find a way to cope and if this means change, then change it is. Survival has been challenged before; a virus will not beat us ... we will beat it! Life will continue; it may not be the life we knew before Covid 19, but this may signal a new beginning in which acceptance and a new challenge awaits us, where we hopefully will emerge happier, wiser and more authentic than ever before. As 'heroes', our journey begins with the end of 'normal' as a new awakening greets us.

I am secretly pleased to have lived through a pandemic, as it has given me an insight into what our forebears must have suffered in years gone by. One big difference, however, is that we have a government that has pumped millions of dollars into the economy to help us survive financially. This was not so for our predecessors, who struggled to rebuild the country's economy without financial help and for this we must feel truly grateful!

Being near the end of my life cycle, I will not be affected as much as the younger generation, but they must face reality and make changes to suit a new life that awaits them. Technology will be a key player in the future, online shopping will take off and become the new norm. Exciting new careers lie ahead for those who are willing to embrace the future with enthusiasm.

Back to lockdown

Today my bulbs arrived that I ordered online from Nichol's Garden Centre. They were delivered by a Nichol's van. I nearly died when I saw the large bag of bulbs I must have ordered. I have never shopped online for anything other than clothes, so this was a first! It won't be the last; how easy is it to go online and order, then have them delivered, hassle free? This meant work, as I had to think where they were going to be planted. This took up most of the afternoon as I walked around my garden plotting as to where to bury them. Next morning, I came up with a solution. I would plant some of them in old plant containers that were lying around (tidily, of course), then I would just place them in my garden when they were in bloom. How good was that?

As a resident was passing, she called me aside to tell me of a funny incident that had happened in her household. She had to take a photo of her husband's knee and send it through the internet to his doctor. She asked him to remove his trousers, which he did with a protest, as he was worried someone might come to the door and see him in his undies. She annoyingly assured him that his bulge was in the right place, what was the worry? She squatted down to take the photo and set the phone up so as to get the perfect shot. Once that was done, she sent it through to the doctor who was waiting for it. His reply came back, "That is a nice photo, but where is the knee?", and when she pulled it up, much to her surprise there was a photo of her! The camera had been facing the wrong way and it was a photo of her squatting, nothing to do with her husband. And they say oldies don't have fun.

At last our friends from Alexandra have shifted into their cottage in our village. They were ready to move in, but of course the lockdown shattered their plans, so their life was put on hold. But five weeks later they have finally arrived. The furniture truck arrived to pick up their furniture from their home and they were surprised to see a smaller van than they expected. This, of course, led to chaos, as they couldn't get all the furniture in, so had to leave some behind. Also, their beloved cat had escaped from his box and couldn't be found so they had to leave without him. This was not a good experience as the removers were rough when placing their furniture into their cottage, so they were happy to see the last of them. Now it is a waiting game to see when the rest of the furniture arrives. And then there is the problem of their cat. A neighbour is keeping her eye out in case it comes back, when she will catch it and put it into a cage. But in spite of all this, they, like us, know they have made the right decision.

This Sunday morning as my soul mate and I were enjoying a little sun, our neighbour popped his head over the fence and told us he had spent the morning rearranging his furniture. "I've got a cabinet in the corner that annoys me so I'm going to get rid of it. I think I will donate it to the men's shed," he said. We talked a little longer then lunch time was upon us. Later in the afternoon I met him again as he was just coming back from his walk, but he had his walking stick instead of his walker. "I'm going to have a sit down as I am tired." "Where is your walker?" I asked him. "It's too darn noisy, it annoys me. I hate the plastic wheels, they make too much noise." "No wonder you are tired, after moving your furniture this morning and now your walk. You certainly deserve to put your feet up," I told him in a stern voice. "But guess what? I pulled the cabinet to bits and now I have a new occasional table," he concluded. This dear soul is ninety-four years young; he is a real honey!

On my walk I stopped to talk to the new arrivals, to see if all was okay with them. While we were talking the marathon man was briskly walking past so I introduced him to them and explained that they would see him passing by five times each day. I had tried to visualise his age, but because of his briskness I could not even hazard a guess. There was only one way to find out and that was straight from the horse's mouth. He willingly told us his age and we couldn't believe it; I would never have put him in that age bracket. It gives me faith that one day I might be able to walk even just once around the village perimeter without my crutch, as I have another ten years of practice before I reach his age. Hope is on the horizon!

Monday again, where did the week go? The sun has come out, so many residents are tidying up their gardens as the rubbish bin is getting a pounding. If the glass recycling people don't appear soon, we will all have to cease drinking, as there is no room left in the bottle bin, it is overflowing! Wine bottles seem to be the problem, but in times of hardship, or should I say in times of lockdown, many of us turn to the bottle and why not? The alternative is to swallow a calm-me-down pill to take away the worries of the world, but a swig of wine or port is a better solution ... well, a more enjoyable one! (But not excessively, just in moderation, of course!)

Tuesday, 5 May 2020 was a shocking day weatherwise, but Covid 19 brought about its second day with no new cases, which gave us all hope that we were on the right track towards recovery. Today, Wednesday, we watched the one o'clock broadcast by the Prime Minister on how Level 2 was going to work. It opens up our lives again and we will feel by doing our lockdown time, we have contributed to making this step possible when it comes to fruition. Please hurry!

While sitting on my tell-all seat today, Thursday, my mind was jogged by a passing resident who several months back approached me at the local supermarket. I was hobbling on my crutches making my way to the delicatessen counter to buy my week's supply of salmon, while my soul mate was perusing his favourite lolly aisle. While the resident and I were standing in line, he said to me, "Do you mind if I ask you a personal question?" My mind quickly went into overdrive. What on earth was he going to ask me? 'I know,' I said to myself, 'he is going to ask me my age,' so I was prepared. Instead this is what transpired: "How on earth do you manage to paint your toenails?" I nearly did a backflip; this was not what I was expecting. I burst out laughing and answered, "With much difficulty, but I manage!" I couldn't believe that he had noticed my painted toenails. Of all the questions he could have asked me and it had to be about my feet? I didn't know if I should have felt disappointed or jubilant. But in saying this, I love painted nails, both fingers and toes, always have and always will.

This incident reminded me of something that happened while we were on a cruise to Japan. One day while sunbathing on the top deck a lady walked by and stopped at my side. She was looking at my legs. How rude, I thought, then she said to me in a real American drawl, "What lovely feet and toes, have you insured them?" I immediately sat up not knowing how to handle this, but did it in the only way I knew when caught off guard: I burst into laughter. "I am serious," she answered. Perhaps she was an insurance agent trying to drum up business to pay for her cruise. I promptly picked up my belongings and disappeared, not wanting to hang around in case she had other ideas.

Another Friday without happy hour, oh how I miss this gathering, but surely it can't be far off now? Please, please, make it happen soon! We need our freedom, we are like caged animals. Because it is miserable today, I settle down with a book, given to me by a kindly neighbour. It was written by a resident in our village. It was memoirs of his and his partner's life. It held my attention; such a talented couple, so well travelled, what an exciting life they had experienced. Most people including myself would only have dreamt about the places they visited and the shows they attended. I was fascinated with where they had been, where they had lived, and the worldly people they had mixed with! They lived a very public life, which showcased their flair for building up successful businesses from the foundation up. He wrote with deep passion and from one author to another, I know how it feels to sit day after day, month after month and reach an end result that one is proud of. It gives back a feeling of achievement and pride. We have another something in common: we are both artists!

Last night I watched the TV programme *Rebuilding*

Paradise with Paul Henry. Although Paul is a 'smarty pants', he interviews some interesting people. From last night's interview I picked up on several phrases that I thought were important. They related to what we are all experiencing and what we are going to face in the future: 'semi freedom at Level 2', 'we have to think from go to whoa', 'this crisis is larger, longer and deeper than anything we have ever experienced' and 'forward into the future we have to re-invent ourselves and our lives'. But his interview with Kelvin Davis, the Minister of Tourism, was a disaster. Paul's bolshiness was overpowering, making the minister look like a lost soul searching for answers, to which he had none. Then he had the cheek to cut him off with a hasty goodbye. Politics is a cruel business, one I would stay well clear of! I can but only admire our Prime Minister for the way she has conducted herself through this crisis, but I beg of you, Jacinda, let Level 2 happen next week: we need our freedom and people need to work.

An alien world!

There were two more cases of Covid 19 today. For the first time in six weeks I had to venture to the supermarket, as our trusty shoppers forgot to get my bread (a good excuse to break free). It was great to get behind the wheel again and exert my power! But what greeted me was far from the life I once knew.

I had to join the line of shoppers all waiting to make it through the supermarket door. This I remembered from my last visit, but what came next, I was not expecting. When it came time for me to proceed, a man signalled for me to enter so I dutifully went through the door only to find no trolleys in the foyer, where they used to be. "Excuse me, where are the trolleys?" I asked him. "You walked past them; they are all outside." This meant I had to backtrack outside once again. I picked out a trolley and had to go to the back of the queue and start the process all over again.

Once in the supermarket and with the hand sanitiser applied, I went about my shopping in my usual manner. It wasn't until I was halfway through my shopping that I spotted a sign at the beginning of the aisle saying 'Wrong way', then I looked down at the floor and saw a huge black cross. Oh my God, again I had sinned. I was not obeying the rules, no wonder people were looking at me. I thought they were pitying me because of my crutch and trying to manoeuvre the trolley, but instead they probably thought, she is a bird-brain! Once I had familiarised myself with what was expected, I continued on with the deed at hand.

Now it was time to make my way to the counter to pay. To my surprise the queue was so long, it was back to the waiting game where one had to stand on the green crosses. One could have been forgiven thinking they were young again, back to the noughts and crosses era. By this time twenty minutes had passed before I was signalled to proceed to checkout. The lady before me was paying for her groceries so I started to unload my trolley onto the counter when I was severely told off. "Just a minute, lady, you are meant to be standing on the cross until I call for you to proceed. I have to sanitise the counter after each customer." Once again, I felt stupid and put in my place. Was I in fact safe out of the village on my own? I began to doubt myself. Was this the new norm? Then I thought back to the phrase 'we have to re-invent ourselves'; is this

MEMORIES AND MOVING ON

where it had to start? I climbed into my wagon and thought to myself, 'I went to the supermarket elated and have come home deflated!'

Although it is only Saturday, the day before Mother's Day, our daughter and her partner rang to say they were on their way over to ours with four dozen fresh oysters. Would I make some batter? This was their Mother's Day shout. The men were in the lounge talking and we were busy draining the oysters when my daughter told me to grab a couple of raw oysters and she did the same. They were delicious! Then I saw her cutting some oysters in half. "What are you doing that for?" I asked. "The guys will know we are oysters short, so if I halve some then we will still get our dozen each." "You devious little minx," I told her. I learnt then that we can all learn by the younger generation; they are right up there with all the tricks of the trade! In all we had a lovely night; the oysters were delicious, although a remark was passed about the size of some of them, I wonder why?

Today was actually Mother's Day and a lot more movement was going on in the village, as children visited their parents. We all knew the two-metre rule and abided by it, where possible. My soul mate had a terrible night, visiting the toilet many times and woke up feeling sick, so he stayed in bed. He tried to blame the oysters, but the rest of us had survived so it wasn't them. But in saying that, I forgot a conversation I had with a couple yesterday: when telling them we were having oysters for tea, they asked if my soul mate was allowed to eat shellfish. People on chemo medication were not meant to eat shellfish apparently; this we never knew, so perhaps this was the cause.

On my walk this afternoon I met up with a couple who had taken a break and were resting on seats by the bowling green. They were in conversation with another resident who had been given a pot with flowering tulips for Mother's Day. I couldn't believe that tulips were flowering already as I had just planted my bulbs. But it was explained to me that the growers trick their bulbs into a false season by growing them under lights for twenty-four hours a day. It was even suggested that if a paper bag was put over the bud before it flowered you would get a pale green flower. The couple had been to Holland a few years ago and seen the beautiful tulips, dwarf ones as well as standard, and in such an array of colours.

With each day one learns new things; we never stop learning as life never stands still. To still be gathering knowledge as one grows older keeps us positive and alert, along with a purpose to get up and keep going to seek what the new dawn will teach us. Let us gain all the knowledge that is available to us! I love life and am eager to learn all I can, this is my inquisitive self. But there are many good things that come from being inquisitive and curious; you find all you need to know, straight from the horse's mouth! An article appeared in the 'Mix' supplement, stating that curious people have a positive and resilient mind and are genuinely happy people. It can also help our brain against memory loss (sometimes I question this).

Today is the big day we have all been waiting for, Monday, 11th May. The decision by our Prime Minister to let us know if we are moving from Level 3 to Level 2. Are we going to be happy or disappointed?

There were three new cases of Covid 19, which cast a little doubt whether we would move down. But at four o'clock we were all told of the great news: we are moving to Level 2 at 11.59 pm on Wednesday, 13 May. This brought a feeling of elation, suddenly all the suffering we had gone through had helped the Prime Minister make the right decision. Now we were free to visit our friends; instead of talking outside we could go into their homes and share that closeness that had been taken from us. I don't know about the supermarket; I may need a guide to point out the dangers that lurk there. Can I be trusted?

During a conversation a couple of days ago one of the ladies from the village mentioned that she thought the Director-General of Health, Dr Ashley Bloomfield, was wonderful. I suggested she buy one of the tote bags with his image on, then she would have him with her at all times. But she protested saying she didn't want him on her arm, she wanted a T-shirt so he could be close to her chest. How sweet or sexy was that? This proves that we still have feelings no matter what age we are; we just need that little awakening and forgotten feelings are lovingly restored. So, Dr Bloomfield, you have made one lady (along with many others) very happy. When she reads this, she will know who she is, and so will her friends, who were privy to this conversation.

A learned neighbour from along our street dropped by with a booklet on mushrooms and toadstools, which she left for me to read. I now know that the fungi growing on the village green were indeed toadstools, not mushrooms as first thought. This put things straight for me as earlier in my story I mentioned that I was confused as to whether they were mushrooms or toadstools. They are an introduced species to New Zealand and are associated with pine trees, oaks, silver birch or sweet chestnuts. Its correct name is *Amanita muscaria*. *Amanita* is the genus to which most dangerously poisonous species belong to. So, don't be tempted to pick them when gathering wild mushrooms for food. Leave red- and yellow-topped toadstools well alone!

Thursday, 14 May — semi freedom!

Level 2 has arrived and we are now on our third day of no new cases of Covid 19. How good is that? This is a goodbye to our faithful shoppers as now we are able to do our own shopping. So, I along with all the residents would like to say a big 'thank you' to the 'fab four'. Without you we would probably have starved, but in writing this I realise it was within your interest to keep us alive, otherwise no residents, no income. And you did give us some laughs re the interpretation of some of the items requested, as they were different to ours. In saying this, we were all very well looked after, so to you, our 'heroes', another big thanks!

Today the cars that have been parked up for six weeks were taken for an outing. Most went somewhere; did they in fact think we had forgotten them? But from here on, they will be 'on the road again' taking us to an alien world that awaits us; queues of people outside shops, someone telling us when to enter a building, sanitisers, arrows and crosses to follow. For my specialist appointment next Monday at 12.30 pm, I received a text today telling me I have to wait in the car in the hospital car park until I get a phone call, then by myself I have to go to Suite 3, where I will be seen. Is this the uncertainty of the new normal? Is this where we have to pause and reset the way we live?

Will we be able to adjust? The answer has to be a positive 'yes'. We must abandon our former collective illusions, as we are never going back; we will bounce forward with better, fairer and more passionate views on life. It will take time for us to feel normal again. The uncertainty of a new normal awaits us, as it is impossible to say where we are going. We have to build and reconnect with wisdom and strength within ourselves, then move forward in a time of trial and transformation; hopefully with a renewed focus on health and wellbeing, our environment and cultural values. Let us not forget who the 'heroes' were in our time of need, the underpaid health-care workers, cleaners and supermarket staff. Our focus must shift to remember those who made life so much better for us in this pandemic. Heroes have always been thought of as sportspeople, but our true 'heroes' are ordinary everyday people who were there for us in a time of need.

Today is Thursday, Budget day, so on went the TV to see what the finance minister, Mr Robertson, had to say. He spoke very well and handed out money to many busi-

MEMORIES AND MOVING ON

nesses and areas where it was needed most. One cannot criticise about where the money should go, as no one knows what the future holds for any of us. The government will come under criticism as not everyone will feel happy, but who would want to be in their position? We are moving into an unknown chapter in our lives, so let us believe that it has been handled in everyone's best interest!

Once again, no Friday happy hour, instead a friend invited me and several others to her cottage, to prepare for the resuming of next Friday's happy hour. We had to have a trial run. There was laughter aplenty, the afternoon ran into early evening, the food was tops, we even forgot we had a home to go to, anyway who needed to go anywhere? We were having such a great time. Then of course my book came up and one lady assured me that she wouldn't get a mention, but she is in for a surprise because she has earned her place in history (sorry, in my book).

When it was time to leave, I snuck out her back door while she stood and watched to see I got home safely. I came in through our back door only to find my soul mate was entertaining visitors. I had consumed two glasses of red wine, but I felt I had drunk a whole bottle. I was out of practice because of the potent painkillers I am on at the moment, they don't mix at all well with alcohol. Never mind, I felt relaxed and had a great night's sleep.

Earlier today I sussed out the Dunedin company that designed the image of Dr Ashley Broomfield for the tote bags and T-shirts, as I wanted to buy one for his fan from our village. I rang, but unfortunately, many other women had the same idea so they were sold out as they went to print. They had a licence to print only so many, and once that order was fulfilled, production stopped. The money from this merchandise went to a charity. So, my dear friend, I'm sorry I couldn't get you the T-shirt; not even a tote bag was available, so you will just have to keep an image of Dr Ashley Bloomfield in your mind, instead of across your chest!

A week has passed and we have had only two Covid 19 cases in seven days. Our good behaviour during Level 2 lockdown is paying off. Today I was speaking to one of our star grocery shoppers and she told me of another incident over the mix-up of a grocery list. Having got down to the last item on a resident's list, she could not decipher what this was, so decided to go with her gut feeling. She purchased a dozen of maxi-beer; she was a little perplexed as she didn't associate beer with this lady, but told herself, it was none of her business what people did in their own cottages. Upon delivering these items to this resident, as soon as she saw the beer she said, "I didn't order beer?" "Then what was the last item on your list?" she asked. "I ordered a dozen Buzz Bars." The beer was quickly returned to the supermarket and one dozen Buzz Bars were purchased and delivered.

Guess what? Friday, 22 May and happy hour has resumed. Tables were set up with six chairs at each table so as to keep our social distancing. It was interesting to see who the eager-beavers were; I was one of them! Plenty of laughter rang out, the management must have been happy to see us all back, as drinks were on them, so a huge 'thank you'. Things are gradually getting back to a new normal, as most activities are returning this week. Hooray!

Tonight, as I was watching *Seven Sharp*, I was thrilled to see a young lady making earrings and pins of popular people. When I saw that she had included Dr Ashley Bloomfield, my mind went into overdrive. Here was my chance to purchase a pin for the resident who thought of him as her hero. It wasn't a T-shirt or a tote bag, but it was the next best thing, so I got on to my computer and purchased one. I'm sure she will be happy with this little memento. I can't wait for it to arrive!

When hope materialises

Today my faith was restored. I mentioned that several months ago I had purchased online, three tops from China. Because they hadn't arrived, I looked up in the scam files and found the company's name listed. Although it was listed a little differently to the one I had sent money to, I was convinced I had been scammed. As the weeks slipped by, this became a reality, so I had given up, vowing never to purchase anything from China again; once bitten, twice shy! But today everything changed.

The post lady delivered a parcel and I was surprised when I saw on the package that it was from China. Surely this wasn't my tops, the ones that I thought I would never see? I brought it inside and on opening the parcel, there they were, so what I thought was a scam was legitimate, what a welcome surprise. My daughter was adamant that I had been caught, but I held on to hope; she said I was clutching at straws. I couldn't wait to tell her my good news. I even felt quite smug! The tops were everything I had hoped they would be, so the saying 'If it looks too good to be true, then it probably is' doesn't always ring true. I had no idea of their sizing in China, so I ordered three sizes larger than I would normally buy in New Zealand and they were a perfect fit. The clothes were quite funky, so different to what one would buy in our country, and the prices were unbelievably cheap.

I have often written about the slave labour and how the girls and women are treated in the sweatshop factories in poor countries, making clothes for the high-end fashion houses, who then sell at highly inflated prices. Now these workplaces are selling through the internet to overseas buyers straight from their factories, which means the middle man doesn't get a bite at the cherry, thus the affordable prices. I do feel a little guilty not buying local, but then I think about the factory girls and how grateful they are to have sewing jobs, as this is how they feed their families. This is their only way of surviving the harsh reality that they face. The only other choices that these poor country girls have are as bar hostesses or, worse, that of prostitution. So, what is the happy medium for our poorer nations? A little support is sorely needed.

Our first night back at cards, hooray, although at a different venue, as the care home is still out of bounds. No one knew how to work the gas heater, so we shivered our way through the night. I must admit I really missed cards, first as a social outing and second as a test of my skills. It was nice to catch up with the players again as we all still have that competitive streak within us. Although if you are not dealt good cards, skill is not a factor, it is just plain bad luck! The saying 'You are only as good as the hand you are dealt' is so true. We welcomed a new player to our group and plenty of laughs were had. The outside temperature was zero degrees so we had a brisk walk home to our cottages. In all, it was a great night.

Late this afternoon we drove into town, as I had to return then exchange a purchase at Farmers department store. It took ages to find someone to help me as I walked around the shop searching for a salesperson. Then I had to go to the cashier counter where there was a long line of customers. Shopping in the 'new now' is certainly not for anyone in a hurry, nor for an impatient buyer. I just presume staff are working at a reduced level as there was only one checkout working. I then made my way out of the department store to pay for my parking. Having entered my card in the right slot, I then tried to put my $20 note in to pay my $4 parking fee, but it kept getting spat out. A young lad, about twentyish, came to my rescue and offered to pay the $4, of which I protested, but as much as I tried to re-insert my money, it was refused. In the end I had to be humble and accept the help offered to me by this kind young man. My faith in mankind had been restored and my heavy heart was suddenly enlightened to know there is still kindness lurking in the younger generation towards the elderly!

Friday today, 29 May, and zero Covid 19 cases for one week, just one active case left in our country. How good is that? The sun shone with this good news so we shared in its good fortune. It is that time of the week again that we all look forward to ... 'happy hour'. It is a good excuse to dress up and celebrate with our fellow residents. We all have stories to tell and share plenty of laughs. We just have to remember, when it ends, where we live, and negotiate our way home safely. But after only two wines, which most of us ladies have, except on the odd occasion when we let our hair down and slip in an extra glass, we seem to have no problems remembering where our grass roots lie! The wonderful thing about village life, we don't have to worry about being mugged while walking home; as the saying goes, 'There is safety in numbers'. One thing for sure, if someone was after money from our purses then they would probably starve to death as there wouldn't even be enough for them to buy a loaf of bread!

Today, Sunday, another lovely day so after cleaning the car I sat in my tell-all seat and started to write. My peace was disturbed by a voice saying, "Don't draw her attention," which was directed at me. There on the road were the likely three, no, actually four today, two with walkers and two with walking sticks. I let them know I could hear them coming and one lady replied, "It was probably me and my big mouth," to which the leader of the pack promptly told her she also had a big bum. "I'm glad I'm not walking in front of you," I told her, to which she answered, "Yes, I would probably tell you that too!" That was me put in my place. Then there was a discussion: would they have a cuppa at someone's cottage? After much deliberation they finally came up with an answer: 'yes'. Really, was it that hard to come up with a simple 'yes'? Older people amuse me. (I forget every now and again that's why I am here, because I'm old, but I'm still young at heart.) I kid myself that I'm just a chicken in a coop with a lot of mother hens. How I wish, but then we all want to pretend we are younger than our age belies!

This morning we had a belated 'Mother's Day' morning tea for all the village ladies. Belated because of Covid 19 lockdown. Our bright, cheerful activities lady did us proud, the tables were all set up with a cut-out pram at every setting, each hiding a chocolate surprise inside. It was tastefully done. Then the jokes started; they were read out by Deborah and set a happy mood around the room. She told everyone about my new book that had just been released, that it was available in the Brooklands library. Next, out came the morning tea on pretty layered cake plates: sandwiches and a selection of cream cakes, this was the icing on the cake. Our manager and his father were our 'billy boys' in the kitchen; they did a wonderful job, a big thanks to you both. In all, everyone enjoyed themselves, as this was our first celebration outside of lockdown. May many more follow.

On this day, Friday, 5 June, for fourteen consecutive days we have had no new cases of Covid 19. But now another issue has arisen that is dominating our world. Emotions are running high regarding racial injustices ... injustices that we are witnessing across our world today. This has been brought about by the brutal death of George Floyd, an African American who suffered at the hands of four ruthless police officers. Rioting has been rampant throughout the US as everyone feels the pain, which is justified. Rallies against this type of brutality have been held throughout the world as racial injustices will no longer be tolerated. Up until now it has been happening, but no longer! Has this been brought about by Covid 19? We all suffered together through this pandemic, have we changed? Are we becoming more united?

Is this the building of a new future where people will no longer stand by and see brutality and grave injustices done to innocent people? This was usually confined within the US, but the whole world came on board and forced the authorities to name, shame and punish the perpetrators for their part in this hideous crime. Because they were police officers, did they think they could take the law into their own hands and not be punished?

All Americans deserve to be treated as equals, regardless of race. No any one person is better than the next. Colour does not define who we are, we are all born equal, so we must begin to live as one nation. Discrimination should play no part in our modern world. Since Covid 19 became part of our lives, is this not a message sent to us by a higher force, to change our old ways, as the world is not the same any more? We must recognise and understand that none of us looks alike, we are all individuals with characteristics of our own. In the end we are all one! Let us adopt a new attitude and start caring for each other. Our world is changing, people of all nations are mingling, therefore a mixed race of people will emerge and we shall experience more diverged cultures.

Monday, 8 June 2020

Today the sun shone down upon us with warmth in its rays, helping us to enjoy what was going to be a new beginning. This is a significant date, in fact a date for us all to remember, as from 11.59 pm tonight we come down to Level 1. This is because five million New Zealanders all pulled together to make this possible, by following rules set out by our Government. We are now seventeen days free of Covid 19. We have no active cases and all sixteen clusters are now closed. Twenty-two deaths have been recorded and in total we had 1504 confirmed cases. This is day 75 of being in a Covid level. From midnight tonight all restrictions are lifted and apart from our border closures with other countries, we will begin our 'new normal', whatever that may be! No one knows what confronts us, many jobs have been lost and many businesses may not re-open. But for one moment, let us celebrate, may we feel joy in our hearts that we got through this pandemic relatively unscathed. Tomorrow is a new day! We can touch and hug once again; this important closeness that has been taken from us, for what seems like a lifetime, is now allowed. How we have missed physical touching with loved ones outside our bubbles. To those people who have lost family members, our thoughts are with you.

Our new focus is the world as it might become. There are no future clues to that and there is no history to guide us. The world is alone! So all of us, as particles of this universe, must support crucial decisions made by higher authorities, as we cannot step aside from the possibility that Covid 19 may at any time return!

While I was sitting in my tell-all seat enjoying the sun, a lady from further down our street came past and we ended up having an interesting conversation about our aging parents. This brought us to thinking about our neighbour Emelie, who just today had moved from her cottage into the care home. We will miss her as she was a sprightly lady who walked every day; she was quiet by nature, but was always around.

As the lady was leaving, she said to me, "I am happy that my neighbour opposite is in competition to you with all your garden bling." This was payback, because a friend from my home town had moved into the village and she was younger than her, so her reign of being the youngest resident had now ended. But in spite of all this, together we won the 'gingerbread house' build at our last year's Christmas party. We were a good team then, now we are sparring partners!

Later this afternoon our mailbox got in someone's way so they ran into it! I heard the bang and saw the car tangled in the now-twisted wreck. The man drove down the street, then alighted to see what damage had been done to his car. He walked up the street and came to our door and apologised profusely for his misdemeanour. I asked him if he was from the village, but he had come from Invercargill to have a look at the village as a friend asked him to check it out. We talked for a few moments and he had a good look around and then asked questions. I gave a good sales pitch, telling him it was the best move we had made and that I loved it here. He was impressed. Hopefully another sale, Tony! Is commission on the cards?

Today was Molly day! As mentioned earlier in my story, Molly had a crush on Dr Ashley Bloomfield; the pin had arrived, now it was time to present it to her. I have taken the liberty to mention her name as it was made public when I did the presentation. At our friendship group morning tea, I made a speech about a resident and her 'crush' on Dr Bloomfield. Then it was time for her to reveal herself so I could attach the pin on her. She had no idea this was going to happen but I knew she would take it all in good heart, as the limelight does not faze her. Molly was delighted as now she had a pin with the new love of her life.

On the way home I ran into the gardener and we had a good laugh when I told him what had happened. He told me Molly had told him that I wrote raunchy books; they weren't really raunchy, just about life as it is. We had a good discussion about her as she is well known around the village. She is a straight-to-the-point person, who is not afraid to voice her opinion. You certainly know where you stand with her, nothing is hidden. I have a lot of time for her in spite of her coming across as the haughty matriarch, but she is quite innocent in a lot of ways and is not beyond enjoying naughty humour. She is a very caring person, which is a lovely quality to have. Molly lives and breathes village life, attending most activities and functions believing that if they are not patronised by the residents, then they will be lost. She is like the cheerleader, rounding up all her girls to partake in all that is on offer. I am happy we ended up in the same street, as she is a real joy, in fact a treasure. There will be residents who think otherwise, because of her outspoken manner, but they would be the least of Molly's worries.

Has our trust been broken?

The day is 16 June and we are heartbroken to learn that we have two new Covid 19 cases in New Zealand, brought into our country by two women who arrived from the UK. They had been given special exemption to attend a family bereavement, only having been in quarantine for less than a week. They then drove from Auckland to Wellington, without being tested when they left the hotel.

The people of New Zealand feel cheated, as five million of us did our bit to get our country Covid free, only to find our good work has been undone! There has been neglect by the authorities to enforce a Covid 19 test on these women before leaving isolation. Have we become too complacent, will this be our undoing?

One day later we have learnt that these two women had contact with friends where hugs and kisses were exchanged. They, in fact, originally denied having made contact with anyone during their trip, now the truth has come out. Where is this going to take us? Hopefully it will not lead to the beginning of another Covid cluster. This has left us with heavy hearts and the waiting game begins once again.

Amid all this confusion a second wave of coronavirus has hit Beijing, the source being Xinfadi Market, similar to the one in Wuhan. They are now back in lockdown to try to contain the virus. All the new cases have been connected to the market, which is now closed and under police surveillance. Tourists and sporting events in other parts of China have now been banned. The areas surrounding Beijing are in a 'wartime emergency mode' and once again the panic has begun.

Meanwhile, the news in our country just gets worse. It was revealed today on 10 June, a day after funeral exemptions were banned, six people who had flown in from Australia were in fact allowed to attend a tangi in Hamilton. The ministry did not say whether the people were tested before leaving. Also, mourners at a wake in Auckland expressed surprise that a person who stepped off a plane from a Covid hotspot, just a day earlier, was allowed to attend the event without having been contacted by authorities! What has happened to our government? Have they let their guard down because we had so many days Covid free? We expect better!

Another case of Covid 19 has surfaced today so now

we have three cases. Is this the beginning of a new wave? Tomorrow is another day, so let us hope we receive better news.

Yesterday was Friday, the last day of the week, which a lot of us socialites look forward too. Drinks day! In other words, 'happy hour', where we can don our glad-rags and kick up our heels ... hardly ... a wonderful thought though. All we can do is tell a yarn or two and have a good laugh and enjoy each other's company. Our faithful barman is always there to welcome us with a smile; he knows what we all drink, he has us off pat. There are the ones he has to watch, in other words the ratbags. Am I one of those? I wonder!

We walked down with our elderly neighbour and met up with other friends; before long there were eight people at our table. We always seem to be the rowdiest table, laughter ringing out aplenty! Our friend took his empty beer bottle up to the barman and told him the contents had evaporated, could he get a new bottle. When he came back this is what he said: "The barman even had the cheek to charge me for a new one." This brought a raft of laughter. 'Happy hour' is an appropriate name for this gathering. Some need a little prodding or an excuse to meet and greet, but not myself or the lady from 'up the hill'; we are great patrons of this exclusive club!

Another day has passed with devastating news. Two new repatriates from India have Covid 19, now we have five cases. Apparently, they were not showing signs of the virus, but the tests revealed they were indeed infected. How can this happen? More cases have taken the number to ten; all are repatriates coming home from overseas, bringing the virus back with them. People are not happy!

Today I was asked to be a guest speaker at a book club outside our village. A resident picked me up in her car and we drove to a member's home. It was a privilege to meet new people who were book fans. They had all brought books along that they had read, now it was discussion time on what they thought of their choices. It was entertaining for me as an author to listen to what they had to say, as I was able to pick up on a couple of things that I could give advice on later.

It was my time to shine! I told them why I entered the writing world and the joy it brought me. Now the pitfalls ... one could not make a living from writing, as it is very competitive. To get a publisher was almost nigh on impossible for new writers, as the publishers have their loyal writers who keep pumping out new novels. Why change a winning formula? But to us newbies, we feel cheated!

The most significant point that came under discussion was the number of words — sixty thousand — before a book could be classified as a novel. One lady said she could now understand why some books are full of descriptions rather than keeping the momentum flowing, which she thought digressed from the story. I understood where she was coming from as I had experienced the same problem while reading a specific novel. I didn't want to know what way the leaves were blowing and where to, it seemed irrelevant to the story! Another lady mentioned about the foul language used, which she found a turn-off, as it had no reason to be there, perhaps other than to build up the word count, now that she knew the writer needed sixty thousand words. In all, it was a very enjoyable afternoon.

As every good writer knows, to the public it looks effortless when reading a book, but it only looks that way because the author has put a lot of effort into it! I write because it brings me joy ... it does not bring me money. But as I have learnt over the years, you cannot purchase joy, it comes from within, you earn it by doing something that resonates in your heart. It is easy to work hard and put things out there and then it all disappears into oblivion, so whatever happens, happens! My goal is to create new stories and make people happy.

Today I took a copy of all my novels, nine in all, to the Mosgiel Library as a donation. Now they are available for people who have met me and want to read them. It is no good my promoting my books if they are not available for the people I have spoken to.

This morning I managed to find time to fulfil a promise to a resident. She had asked me to come to her cottage and help sort out her wardrobe as she could not reach the top shelf. It was fun sorting through her clothes, as it made me realise that I wasn't the only one who purchased items of clothing only to put them away, out of sight, out of mind! We found plenty of surprises that were still in their bags; clothes she had forgotten about, along with handbags. It was like shopping in one's own wardrobe. I arranged them on the shelves so they could be seen at a glance, nothing was hidden, everything was now out in the open. I told her she had a lot of years' living to do, to get the use from her clothes, otherwise this was a wasted exercise! She was happy, I was happy for her, so we were two happy chappies. What more could one wish for?

Disaster strikes at home

My soul mate and I have had a week from hell. It all started when a household utensil attacked me in my kitchen. I had bought a new grater as my old one was past its use-by date. It was a lovely shiny one, an upmarket one; well, an upmarket-priced one. It was one you held in your hand and just ran the vegetables down the sharp grates. Today, as I was grating cheese, my finger must have got in the way so it ended up with skin missing from the tip. I quickly bandaged it and bravely carried on until I felt a sharp pain and then a sea of blood followed. My hand had slipped and my thumb knuckle was minus the skin down to the bone, no wonder there was pain and blood. When my soul mate saw the damage, he opened the door to throw the grater away, but I promised him I would pension it off. New it might have been and an expensive designer one at that, but it was a lethal weapon, one that was not going to grace my kitchen any longer!

Then the next day while at Smiths City store in Dunedin my soul mate wandered off to have a look at some heaters. I saw a cushion that was a perfect match for the rug on the lounge floor, so made my way to the counter. I spoke to the salesperson saying I wanted to buy one and he said to me, "Why not buy two as you get them for the price of one?" What would my soul mate say as he has a pet hate for cushions? One I could justify, but two, was that pushing it too far? I replied, "Oh really, I would be silly if I didn't," so two it was. Suddenly I heard a loud thump and saw shop attendants rushing to where the noise had come from, so I joined them only to find my soul mate lying on the floor. I panicked; was this karma for my buying two cushions? He was helped to sit up until he got his bearings, as he was in shock. Then they lifted him to his feet. I held on to him but he assured all of us he was okay. It wasn't until a few hours later the pain started in his rib area on which he had fallen, which probably meant he had bruised or cracked his ribs. Three days later he is still in pain, so we are a sorry pair. Looking on the bright side, things can only get better.

Today we have a total of fourteen active Covid cases, but thank goodness there is no community transmission; all are expatriates coming home. I have been one of those who have been annoyed that these cases have been brought in from overseas. But on listening to a young man on television last night explaining why it had taken him so long to come back to New Zealand, it made me stop and think about being so judgemental; after all, this is his homeland. Where would I want to be if caught up in a crisis? Back in my own country, of course.

Another week has gone by and we now have twenty-one Covid cases. There has been an outbreak of cases in Melbourne so it looks like the borders will not be opening any time soon. My soul mate and myself were meant to be leaving on 18 July for a month in Australia but Jetstar cancelled our flights and as the borders will not be open, we can wave goodbye to our holiday! Thank goodness we had taken insurance out on our accommodation. Jetstar will not refund our fares, and we have to re-book within a year.

Today a friend and I went on a bus tour with the 'Sunshine Travel Club', who came to the village and picked up six residents. This was the bus company's first tour since lockdown and they had so many requests, therefore needed two buses, which was great. Richard, the owner, owns three bus companies and told us they had suffered financially, so they now only had one company that was viable. Since the talk of no cruise ships coming until 2023, this was a big hit on them. I did not realise the toll this pandemic had taken on local companies until Richard explained this to us. He had to lay off drivers and an office lady so the company could survive.

Our tour was to Port Chalmers then around the corner

to the Carey's Bay Hotel for a top-notch lunch. We were graced with Eric, the only man at our table, but he was no trouble, in fact he was as quiet as a mouse, but then he was swamped by us womenfolk. Most of our table ordered fish and chips for our main, including Eric, then we ordered separate desserts. Before we started our main, several platters were brought to our tables, so of course we had to have a wine, this was par for the course! The lunch was good value and most enjoyable.

Then it was time to get on our bus and carry on to Aramoana. We climbed onto the bus only to find our seats were taken. It was then pointed out to us we were on the wrong bus, so we had to retreat back the way we came. No, it wasn't the wine as we only had one glass each; it took more than one glass to obscure my memory. Never mind, this was an added laugh.

We then continued on to Aramoana where we were going to walk down the spit and see the seals. As we pulled up, Richard opened the bus door and in blew the cold wind and several drops of rain, so we all yelled out 'no', we didn't want to do the walk as it was bitterly cold. So, we enjoyed the view from within the bus. The second bus followed suit; they were 'boobs' like us, as no one wanted to brave the weather. On the way home Richard took a detour around the port to where all the logs were stored to go overseas. There were millions of them; the port wanted rid of them to make more room for containers, so they were going to be transported up to Dunedin where the ships would have to go to load. It didn't seem to make sense, but then I'm not into logs so what do I know?

The trip home was interesting as we had many stops dropping people off at their respective places. In all it was a lovely day, as my friend and I didn't seem to do anything but laugh all day, thus we decided that laughter was the best medicine to fix all ailments. She asked me if I ever felt down, to which I said I had learnt through meditation and self-belief to be happy all the time. I begin each day with a happy heart.

In the future I will be supporting the Sunshine Travel Club in the hope that their business will continue, as it was a great day out and one is 'learning all the time', as comedian Benny Hill would say.

Tonight, I was thinking about our up-and-coming midwinter Christmas dinner and the chosen theme, '1920s style'. What would I dress up as? Perhaps as a flapper or a madam, even a gangster? But then I began to think I was too old to be a flapper and show off my legs, which now resembled strainer posts. A gangster sounded exciting, but then I thought about my big bum in pin-striped trousers, that would be a laugh; so at this stage a brothel madam seemed to be my 'choice of the moment'. I went on to the internet to see what style of wig I could purchase to make me look something along the lines of a madam. It didn't take me long to find the perfect one, so I made a purchase. As I continued looking, I found another wig I fancied; it was a silver bob cut, which would suit a flapper, so another purchase was made. Now I am back to the same scenario: a flapper or a madam? Whatever I decide, I have a choice, one or the other? Decisions make life complicated.

Today, Saturday, 11 July, has been a beautiful day, which was a welcome change after the wet, overcast days of the past week. Last Tuesday we had our Residents AGM and our guest speaker was Sue Bidrose, CEO of Dunedin City Council. Sue talked us through her colourful life with stints overseas, which was interesting to say the least. What a multi-talented lady, who set goals and proved to herself she could achieve positions in all fields of work. Starting with testing cow 'poo' for worms, which had to be tested before it hit the ground so it had to be gotten before it left the cow, poor girl, but this did not deter her. She did counselling and held various other positions before she applied for the position of CEO for the Council. This was her farewell talk as CEO, as she was taking up a new position with AgResearch in Christchurch.

It was interesting to hear her comparing her rate demand for her home in Dunedin, $4,000, to her similar-priced home in Christchurch, $9,000. Sue told us the people of Dunedin had the lowest rates of any city in New Zealand, and were very lucky, as our council was a wealthy council, with a lot of investment properties. I was intrigued to hear this, as there have been many complaints with talk of rate hikes, but we all expect our councils to supply all our needs and wants ... so user pays!

She has a love affair with Dunedin, so has kept her home here and will come back to retire. I found her to be an inspiring person who spoke her mind, and if you didn't like what she said, she wouldn't lose any sleep over it. One gutsy lady going places!

On the not-so-nice side of life were those disrespectful returning Kiwis who were meant to be in isolation, but decided to buck the system by taking the law into their own hands and leaving isolation. I say disrespectful because we have all gone through the Covid 19 levels to make our country safe, then those 'scumbags' come along, who we are paying to keep in top hotels for two weeks and we get 'shat' on. This is not good enough. Most of us are angry over this; they have lived the good life overseas and because they want to return to our 'safe haven' they expect us to keep them. Let us look after the true-blue Kiwis who have lost jobs due to the Covid virus and hire them first. Life seems a bit distorted at the moment, as we still have more hurdles to cross before the real impact is known.

We only have to look at Australia to see how quickly things can change, with so many new Covid cases, in fact 217 today alone. Parts of Melbourne have gone back into lockdown for another six weeks. Borders are closed, with police patrolling them. There was even mention today of a 'cluster' in Sydney, so we shall await more news on this. Let us pray our country stays Covid free. I cannot see the borders between the two countries opening any time soon due to this new outbreak.

'Twas but a moment in time

When I thought my secret romantic dream had turned into reality. Here goes my story! Yesterday was a miserable, wet day and my soul mate, who had not left the house for three weeks because of a fall and a couple of cracked ribs later, decided he wanted to have a little flutter on the 'pokies'. "Let's go to the casino and have dinner there, then you won't have to worry about cooking," he stated. Anything that released me from my kitchen duties was definitely a winner! Into the bedroom I rushed and donned my glad-rags. I don't mind the casino for a short period of time, so to give my soul mate some leeway I asked him to drop me off at the Meridian Mall and I would join him later.

Two hours had passed and I had added to my wardrobe, not that it needed adding to, so now it was time to make my way to the casino. As I was diagonally crossing the main street a downpour happened and I got drenched. I couldn't run as my crutch would not allow this; I hobbled instead. 'Where the hell were all the taxis?' None was in sight. I made my way to the Octagon and as luck would have it, one idle taxi was awaiting me. I climbed in the back seat, drenched as I was, and asked to go to the casino, which was only two blocks away. The poor driver didn't look at all pleased, so I made my play. "You are a life-saver, in fact my hero, thank goodness you came to my rescue." This brought a forced smile. When I alighted from the taxi, which cost me $7.50, I left with these passing words: "This is the best value for money I have spent in ages." Hopefully I had made his day even with such a small fee, but money is not everything; kind words can triumph over money!

Upon meeting my soul mate, he was enjoying himself as the pokies were being kind to him. He gave me some money to have a punt, so away I went. Luck was definitely not with me today; I was down to my last dollar when the machine made a bit of noise and suddenly, I had $110. I had another couple of pushes and then drew my money out. At least I was going home with the same amount I had put into the machines. This is known as a good day at the pokies, to come home with what one started with; anything above this was a bonus. Now it was time to eat.

As my soul mate was paying the cashier, I was standing to his side when I noticed a young man winking at me. Surely this was meant for someone else so I looked behind me, to see who the lucky lady was, but no, there was no one there. I looked at him again and he cast me another wink. He was young and handsome to boot, had my luck changed? Then he made his way over to me. My heart jumped a beat. Did I know him? Did he know me? Then he smiled. "I have been watching you. Your hair, I love the colour," he said in a foreign brogue. I was at a loss for words, but that voice, was he my long-awaited Irish heart-throb who had come to whip me off to a faraway land? But so young? "Are you Irish?" I asked. "No, I am a Welshman," he said, which was why he was hard to understand, but it didn't matter where he came from, he was cute.

As my soul mate turned around, the young man reached out and shook his hand. "I'm pleased to meet you, sir." He was shell-shocked; who was this cocky young whippersnapper? I had a sudden thought: was he going to ask if he could take me away, or even borrow me for however long? That would have been okay, but when the grey roots appeared, what then? Would I be traded for a younger redhead? The young man came closer to me and kept talking about my hair. It was only then I smelt alcohol on his breath; perhaps he had seen an illusion, not the real me? But whatever ... it was but a moment in time! He made me feel desirable again!

That night when I went to bed, his image was still with me. A toy boy, what a wonderful thought! I lay there thinking, perhaps his eyesight wasn't all that good? No, that wasn't fair to him or me. Then perhaps he was after a mother figure, but I was a grandmother, not that he knew that. But whatever ... that wink and smile turned my luck around. It proved one thing to me: dreams can come alive, if for just one moment! That was the up-side, but I have learnt that with an up-side comes a down-side.

I decided to share this special story with my forty-something-year-old daughter. Wrong decision: she burst my happy bubble completely. "He was probably watching you gambling and thought you had plenty of money, therefore would be a soft touch. You are really quite stupid, mother, what young man would look at you?" This was like being stabbed in the back. My happiness quickly vanished, I just wanted to crawl inside my shell and never face reality again. Where was the laugh that I thought we would both share, as my friends and I had done when I told them this story? Then I remembered all I had learnt through meditation. Don't listen to others, don't let anyone put you down or make you feel less than what you are. Listen to your heart, it knows you best. So happiness reigned again!

This morning I was just finishing my meditation when I was suddenly drawn to the fact that a vehicle was leaving our driveway. Oh my God, did someone see me with my eyes closed and my arms reaching up to the heavens? What on earth would they think? No wonder the vehicle was leaving, I had probably frightened them off! Did a madwoman live at this address? As I made my way to the door, there was a parcel placed against the glass. My worst fear: someone had seen me. I opened the door and brought the parcel inside; it was the first of my wigs to arrive. I had been following the tracking number on my computer, so knew it was due any day.

When I ordered them, I thought I was dealing with an American country, but the parcel started its journey in Spain, then to Germany, to Amsterdam and on to New Zealand. I opened it to find the two wigs I ordered last had arrived first, so my first choice wasn't in this bag. Nevertheless I felt excited; reality could disappear and I could become whoever. The world of fantasy was wide open to me. Both wigs were 'boofy' but I was used to a lot of hair, this was me! The first was a black curly shoulder-length one, it was lovely, but the next was silver-grey with curls that reached halfway down my back, it was beautiful. They were of very good quality. Now the fun was about to begin! As mentioned earlier I always had a hankering to own a wig, now I had two with two more to arrive. I went all out when ordering, as this was going to be my one and only wig purchase.

The next morning there was an e-mail on my computer from DHL, the courier company, along with a photo of the parcel sitting on my doormat, as evidence it had been delivered. I began to wonder, had he in fact taken a photo of me in my meditative state, without my knowing?

Two days later the next parcel arrived, so into the

bedroom I ran ripping the bag as I went. There was my first choice, an auburn wig with curls that hung like branches of a weeping willow tree; it was love at first sight. I put it on and stood in front of a mirror. Was this really me? I looked like a haughty madam from the 1920s, just who I wanted to be at the midwinter dinner.

From one story to the next!

This morning as I was talking to my neighbour two cottages down, I told her about the young Welshman, which brought on another wave of laughter. A man from the next street came past carrying a box full of empty bottles. "Do you think you might have a drink problem?" I asked him very cheekily, as he was a man of standing. "They are empty medicine bottles," he informed me. With this exclamation I commented on the size of these bottles. It was time for me to get one back on him as he had accused me of having a gambling problem with the amount of sweepstake tickets I bought on Melbourne Cup day at our Residents Club. Now we were even! Not only is there an out-of-control gambler living in the village but also an over-indulgent medicine man. Residents, beware!

Today we woke to another wet, overcast day. I had a

physio appointment in town, so this filled in the morning. This afternoon I am at a loss as to how to fill in the rest of the day as my trusty computer is no longer trusty, it has packed a sad, so I have sent it off to the computer doctor so it can get a good overhaul. First, he came and tried to fix it but to no avail. I am not good at computer housekeeping, meaning defragging, etc. and other complicated terms, so he took it to his abode where it is residing at the moment. Please may it come back in a better frame of mind and working.

Wow, what a shock at Todd Muller resigning; now we have a new Leader of the Opposition, 'Crusher' Collins. She has the 'balls' to be a strong leader; we don't have to like her, but she has the experience along with Gerry Brownlee. Hopefully they will be a formidable team and pull the National Party out of the doldrums. Now we have two powerful ladies at the top: Aunty Cindy and Aunty Jude. Good luck either way.

As I looked out this morning the ground had been painted white by that wonderful artist Jack Frost. To think I had agreed to go to the friendship group morning tea; just the thought made me shiver. At 9.45 my new best friend and her friend were waiting to pick me up, so I threw on my heavy artillery and on my merry way we went. After we had finished our morning tea it was down to business with Deborah, our witty hostess. Out came the microphone: "Have you all read the brochures you received in the mail on the two referendums you will be asked to vote on at the coming elections?" 'No' was the general consensus. "Well, I will read the disturbing news to you on the cannabis referendum. Do you know because you are over twenty, you can all grow a maximum of four plants per household, as well as have 14 grams of dried cannabis per day in your possession?" This brought hilarity from all us ladies. We could get 'high' on a single glass of wine, imagine the damage if we mixed this with our cannabis allocation. Whose bed would we go home to at night? I suppose as long as we didn't all end up in the same bed, all would be 'okey-dokey' through glazed eyes and a 'wonky' brain. A definite 'no' to this referendum.

The second referendum, 'end of life choice', is a more realistic one for us elderly. In fact, it is important to us as this act gives people with a terminal illness the option to request assisted dying. Most agreed this was a sensible piece of legislation and we all hope it gets a 'yes'. It would be interesting to know how many younger people voted on this referendum as they probably think it doesn't warrant thinking about at their age!

There couldn't be two more outside-the-spectrum subjects to vote on. Giving the young the choice to smoke 'pot', which is still controversial. Imagine driving along the road with a vehicle coming towards you driven by someone who had consumed his quota of 14 grams of 'pot'. It makes me shudder to think what might happen; he might see three vehicles but which one is he going to dodge? Alcohol causes enough damage; do we really need another spanner in the works? The answer is 'no'.

The sun shone today and it was quite warm, not bad for the last week in July. We were holding our midwinter sausage sizzle and concert, so the warmth from the sun brought eighty residents out of hibernation to attend today, which was a great attendance. Mind you, who wouldn't venture out to have lunch cooked for them on the trusty barbecue? Nothing beats a hot snag and onions wrapped in bread with Jim's mother's home-made chutney. The bar was open, manned by our trusty barman, who knows what our choice of tipple is!

After we finished our sausage sizzle, we were entertained by our village ukulele and choir group. Some of the care-home residents were brought over to enjoy the concert. We all sang along merrily to the music; the group were really good, so should be proud of what they have achieved in such a short time due to the Covid lockdown. This was followed by afternoon tea. A most enjoyable day!

Life in the busy lane!

Our street has become a hive of activity, as the builders take to refitting out two vacant cottages. They come in like a demolition crew, ripping the kitchen and bathroom joinery out and chucking it onto the waiting trailer. I was totally amazed watching them turn the inside of the cottages into empty shells. The builders are remodelling and updating with new joinery and new bathroom facilities. On wet days the gardening staff came in and removed all the wallpaper, ready for when the painter arrives. One day we will have two new neighbours, who will move into their newly refurbished cottages and hopefully be as happy as we are. I still can't believe how much I love village life, what a turnaround, but stranger things have been known to happen! I can't name any, but there are bound to be plenty.

Yesterday, Robert the village gardener (I can name

Robert as he is the only male gardener) came to our patch, as I had asked management if I could have a little garden by the back fence, so here he was! My existing garden I inherited and have planted bedding plants and placed ornaments, so now I feel there is a little bit of me here. Along our back fence we have about eight rhododendron bushes that have been there for many years as some are over two feet tall. One of the bushes was very woody so I asked Robert if he would mind removing it for me, to make way for my new piece of garden. I did not believe how he managed to pop it out of the ground. He dug all around it, then drove a crowbar with a hammer underneath the bush, put his weight on the crowbar and out of the ground it popped. I never realised how shallow rooted they are, but then I have never owned a rhododendron bush before, as they would have frozen to death in Central in the winter. This climate is all new to me, in fact a microclimate, I have been told, as I am still buying bedding plants in the middle of winter and they are flowering. Who would have thought? It is almost like a miracle!

Robert asked Mark the builder, who was working across the road, to help him lift it onto the trailer. Now it has been relocated and lovingly restored in Robert's private garden, he is happy, as I am with my newly laid-out garden. Thank you, Robert, nothing is a problem for you, you are a true gem. All that is left for me to do is to unleash my wild imagination, which isn't hard for me, as I am wired up a little different to most people. What a strange creature I am ... exactly, agrees my soul mate!

On the Covid scene, we had nil cases today, but outside New Zealand it is a different story. The virus is rampant throughout the world; Australia had their worst one-day total of 470 positive cases. Where is this virus taking us, as the toll on the retail sector is alarming to say the least? The Warehouse Group has announced it is going to cut 700 jobs and close its non-profiting stores; this along with the aluminium smelter closing and 1500 jobs going spells nothing but disaster for our workforce.

This new world is certainly different to the one we knew before the pandemic came into being. How do we go forward? We are definitely in a dense fog of this long, painful war! Each country is suffering differently, there is no 'one size fits all'. Our world is still in its infancy in the Covid 19 journey. 'Please let us find a vaccine sooner rather than later.' We know little of our future!

I will not be working in my garden this day, as a wintry blast came through last night and left a heavy coating of snow on the Maungatuas as well as a sprinkling on Saddle Hill, so an inside day is inevitable. One minute the sun is out, then its shitty mood brings in rain and sleet showers. How dare it take its vengeance out on us peaceful beings, we have done nothing wrong. Oh well, out comes the pen and pad, now let the writing commence.

My silence has been broken by a funny just brought to my attention on the midday news. It went like this: 'It has been announced that passengers are going to be reduced from six down to five on the gondolas on the Avon River in Christchurch, as one hundred and fifty kilos of meat on a gondola is fraught with danger.' I enjoyed this; it made me laugh at a time when laughs are few and far between!

Another day, another trip

Off I am today on another bus trip, leaving my soul mate home once again on his own. He must wonder who this woman is that pops in and out of this house. But he can't complain; she tucks him up in bed each night, puts his drops in his eyes, then kisses him goodnight. When he gets up in the morning the house is warm, his breakfast is waiting for him, all he has to do is eat it, dry the dishes, then settle down with his morning paper till lunch time. She does his washing and ironing, gets him meals when she is not out, in other words she is his live-in caregiver! In fact, he seems to be happy, as he shares his bed with this 'alien' woman!

Our tour is with the Sunshine Travel Club and we are heading to Kaka Point along the northern part of the Catlins coastline. We stopped at the Kaka Point café to sample their much talked about blue cod meal. It was a rustic old tin and wood building with driftwood aplenty and the sea view was great. All forty-four of us were seated, then the meals started coming out just after we had sat down. The blue cod was so fresh and cooked to perfection, we were all very happy and told the staff so, who in turn thanked us for supporting them in these turbulent times. I realised then, not only were we supporting Richard's bus company, other businesses were also benefiting from us. They are relying on us, the travelling public, to help keep their business up and running, as no one knows what tomorrow will bring.

After lunch we took the coastal drive to the Nugget Point lighthouse car-parking area, where Richard gave us options on what we could do to fill in the next hour. Some elected to walk the one kilometre to the lighthouse, some walked to the lookout point, which was our limit, and some, we won't mention who, decided to rest in the bus. In all it was another pleasant day! As us three ladies from Brooklands Village were the last pick-ups, we were relegated to the back seat of the bus, as that was all the seats that were left. Not that it mattered to us, we could have our laughs wherever we sat.

Thank you to my two companions for your company, let us do this again soon. Oh my goodness, of course next Saturday we are off to Larnach Castle for another midwinter Christmas lunch with Richard. My poor soul mate will be left at home once again; no wonder he shares his bed with me, as this is becoming our only meeting place. My life was never this exciting before coming to live in Brooklands Village.

The big day has arrived, our 1920s midwinter Christmas lunch. I didn't know it took so long to get dressed up for a fancy-dress event, as this was my first, ever! First the black net pantyhose: why do they make them so short in the crutch? By the time they stretched up my not-so-slim legs, the crutch was not where it should have been, which made walking very uncomfortable. I tried many times to stretch them, but when the stretch ran out, I was frightened they would snap, so had to settle for the uncomfortable feel. Then there was the wig: how was I going to hide my curly hair? I scrummaged around in the bathroom and found a shower cap; that would do the trick, I told myself. After shoving all my curls up inside the cap, all was ready to go. On went the wig, with not one piece of my hair to be seen, but to suddenly turn silver, did I suit this look? I was too vain a creature to let my hair go grey, which is why I have multi-colour hair, but this wasn't that awful, in fact it was okay. It had that madam look, and that is who I wanted to be, a madam in charge of all the chorus girls (this is what I will name them); it sounds better than wh.... A sudden change of mind saw me choosing the silver wig over the auburn one as it was more madam-like.

Our friends called to pick us up; they looked awesome, the flapper and the gangster. Together, for several weeks we had waited on our bits and pieces to arrive from overseas. Some did and some didn't make it in time, but it wasn't a big deal. We met up with my new best friend and the five of us merrily made our way to the venue. There was a line of people waiting at the door, as we were asked for the password, then had to be checked off the paid list. No freeloaders were going to gatecrash this party.

What a sight to behold when we stepped inside our Residents Club. Balloons and fairy lights adorned the ceiling and walls and posters banning alcohol were exhibited. There were wanted posters on each table with an image we all knew, but if he was marched off, then the bar would have gone dry. We could not let this happen, besides he looked the part as the dapper barman, so was spared an arrest. The tables were set up with tall thin vases as centrepieces, with fairy lights and huge black and white ostrich feathers exquisitely displayed. Each place setting had a little package and a copy of the *Brooklands Times* dated 29 July 1920, reporting on the doom and gloom of the Great Depression, but this period was also known as the 'Roaring Twenties' — the jazz age — an era of speed, power and glamour.

Our entertainment was a five-piece jazz band, which soon set the mood. Bodies began swaying to the music, then it became too much and the swingers made for the dance floor to let off their pent-up steam. The jazz music was fabulous and mixed with a couple of wines one was transformed back to the 1920s. Much like today with the pandemic, things were as unsettled then as they are now, with an uncertain future as we negotiate our way into the unknown. Thank you for bringing us so much joy for a short period of time.

Local caterers came in and prepared and served the food, which was delicious and plentiful. The meats — beef and ham — were tender, along with roast potatoes and pumpkin, peas and gravy and apple sauce. There were two salads also. Desserts consisted of pavlova, apple crumble, whipped cream and fresh fruit salad. No one would have left feeling disappointed, and if they did, then they are hard to please!

Next came the raffles from which there were ten draws, so ten people were happy; the rest of us made a donation. Deborah and Heather gave us a demo of the Charleston dance along with some brave residents. Time for photos, so we all had a turn in the photo booth, with Deborah as photographer. These photos will be our memories to take away and they will remind us of this wonderful day. We all must have memories to look back on.

Everyone in their own way contributed to today, making it the fun day it turned out to be. A huge thank you to Deborah, Kim, Robert, whoever else, and to our manager Tony, for their time in decorating the Residents Club, so we could enjoy the 1920s theme. Without your contribution the clubroom would never have been the picture it was today. Also, to the management for the beverages, we really appreciate this kind gesture. What a shame it had to end; it was a perfect day, but as the saying goes, 'All good things must come to an end.'

The ending, for real this time!

It is with much sadness I have come to the end of my story, as now it is one year since we came to live at Brooklands Village. I still remember the day we came to measure up for our furniture, when I saw all those residents dressed for '*Titanic* Day' and thought the village was full of old 'fuddy-duddies' and wondered what the hell I was doing coming here. One year on I have joined that group of 'fuddy-duddies' and realise that we are all humans together and have not lost the desire to make life exciting. We have a lot of respect for each other, which is a wonderful quality, but this seems to come with age. I would like to thank all who have been part of my journey, as without you this would only have been half a book. Names of residents have been excluded in most cases, but each of you will know who you are, and if you wish to share your secrets, then that is your choice.

As we grow older, we reach a stage where we form routines, which establishes structure, predictability and some purpose, but this does not mean we can't make changes, so as not to become boring old farts! Nature plays an important part in our lives, it has a positive effect on our health, so let us get out there and enjoy it. Reading and verse are another excellent source of communication, as thinking gives us power, it is stronger than any other instinct. We must seize every moment, as we never know what's around the corner, and we only get one shot at life; there is no plan B, so stick to plan A. Enjoy friends and family and remember to 'laugh out loud' (as I tend to do!).

P.S. It looks like we have the coronavirus contained in New Zealand for the moment; let us pray this is the way it stays in the for-ever future. This is a big ask, as we are alone, this is a new world, there is no guidance as to where we are heading. We are indeed living day by day with hope in our hearts that we will beat this virus and a new 'normal' will prevail. The old 'normal' has gone, it has left us for ever; we have to make new lives from our present situation.

I will leave you with these thoughts on the coronavirus pandemic: 'Was this manufactured to replace a third world war that would have killed thousands of young men in the prime of their lives? Is this pandemic a human replacement to take the lives of the older generation who are nearing their end, to spare these young men a premature death?'

A sobering thought.

Wardrobe attack!

*Yesterday I received a spring catalogue
   in the post,
the clothes were to die for, but the cost
   was upmost?
One particular outfit that took my eye,
was lovely, but the price I couldn't
   justify.
Several of the layers I already owned
and in my wardrobe, they were strewn.
So began the witch hunt to find look-a-
   like substitutes,
that I could put together and cleverly
   execute.
Into this outfit that I loved so much,
all I needed now was a bit of luck?
I was almost there apart from a little
   set-back,
missing was the layer needed in black.
I found a black over-top I forgot I had,
along with a lot of other clothes, I felt
   really bad.
I put together the layers from my own
   shop,
without spending a penny or shedding
   a teardrop.*

*I was in disbelief of this new outfit I
 had created,
now I didn't have to worry, about going
 out naked.
The only difference between the model
 and me,
her outfit was expensive, mine was
 free!*

About the Author

Margaret Nyhon now resides in Brooklands Village, Mosgiel, New Zealand, where she writes, paints and practises the crafts of printing and bookbinding.

She has worked extensively in hospitality management in New Zealand and resort management in Australia. The urge to trace her family history led her to the writing of her first non-fiction work, *de Marisco*. She has since written several fiction and non-fiction works. Margaret is married and has three adult children and two grandsons.

Other books by the author

Non-fiction

de Marisco

Freedom Knows No Boundaries

A Wake-up Call

A Shattered Dream Across the Tasman

Fiction

Isobella (Book 1 in the *Isobella* series)

Isobella: Self Redemption (Book 2 in the *Isobella* series)

Papa's Girl Emmeline

Betrayal by an Irish Rose

Revenge for an English Lord (sequel to Betrayal by an Irish Rose)

For Girls' Eyes Only

Daughters Lost to the Underworld

Pimchan and Amira

www.ingramcontent.com/pod-product-compliance
Lightning Source LLC
Chambersburg PA
CBHW021402290426
44108CB00010B/345